For Mum and Dad

Reminiscence

*Uncovering
a lifetime of memories*

Carmel Sheridan, M.A.

Elder Press
San Francisco
California

Library of Congress Cataloging in Publication Data

Main entry under title:
Reminiscence
Sheridan, Carmel, B.

1. Aged-Home Care 2. Activities 3. Home care services
4. Nursing home care

LCCN 90-083231
ISBN   0-943873-10-X

Printed in the United States of America

Contents

Acknowledgements

I'm grateful for the inspiration provided by all those involved in St. Joseph's day care program in Oakland.

My thanks to the staff of the Vintage Health Resource Library in Berkeley for help in locating useful resources.

To the Alzheimer's Association for their interest and enthusiasm.

To Professor Martin McHugh of the Psychology Department, University College, Galway, Ireland, for his warm encouragement.

To Ellen Koivisto and Eddie for their editorial work.

A special thanks to my family and friends whose support and reassurance were sustaining.

"Very deep ... very deep is the well of the past."

Thomas Mann,
Joseph and His Brothers

Uncovering Memories

What Is Reminiscence?

When we reminisce, we recall memories, review them, and recapture the emotions that went with them. All of us engage in this reflective process from time to time; it is a normal and vital part of growing older.

Why Is It Important For The Elderly?

In later life reminiscence takes on a more significent role: it's how older adults get in touch with things and times that were important to them. Through reminiscing they find meaning in their memories: this helps to maintain their sense of identity, builds self-esteem and helps raise the overall quality of their lives. At a time when older adults may feel vulnerable, isolated or lonely, recalling and communicating their experiences helps to improve their mental, emotional, social and sometimes physical well-being. In reminiscence, older adults have a powerful, natural resource. This book shows you how to help them use it.

9

Benefits Of Reminiscence

Reminiscence by the elderly has all too often been devalued, regarded as a turning away from reality, living in the past and even seen as mental disfunction. We now know, however, that exploring the past is an enriching experience which provides deep personal satisfaction as well as many other important benefits.

- Through the communication and sharing of memories, friendship and understanding are forged; this social interaction heals loneliness and isolation.

- Uncovering and reviewing their memories helps older adults find meaning and purpose in their lives.

- Reminiscence improves quality of life and well-being and raises self-esteem.

- The past is a well of strength for older adults. Drawing on it creates a feeling of security and competence.

- Reminiscence helps resolve conflicts and fears and helps older adults cope with grief and loss.

- In other times the elderly were custodians of culture, heritage, customs and traditions. By relaying family history, ethnic heritage and folklore, today's elderly fulfill a natural and important role. Through this they experience a sense of continuity and intergenerational understanding.

- For the listener, reminiscence has many rewards. There is the satisfaction of being able to help someone; the warmth in getting close to them, enjoying their stories and even learning from their wisdom and experiences. Through this the listener can see her own part in life's journey.

Who Can Benefit From Reminiscence?

The vast majority of older adults will benefit from reminiscence. It's a resource accessible to the broadest spectrum of individuals from the well elderly to those with physical, emotional and cognitive handicaps. Reminiscence is especially beneficial to persons suffering from Alzheimer's disease.

Who Can Use Reminiscence?

Anyone who has regular or repeated contact with the elderly can use reminiscence — family, friends, visitors, social workers, activity directors, occupational therapists, nurses, doctors, clergy and volunteers. Reminiscence can be used in the home, hospital, social center, church, day care and rest home—where ever older adults spend time.

What Is My Role In Reminiscence?

The listener's role in reminiscence is two-fold:

(1) Encourage the older adult to share memories.
(2) Pay active and genuine attention to the reminiscer as memories unfold.

These steps are easily mastered and described in the next chapter.

" There is nothing I like more than conversing with old persons; for I regard them as travelers who have gone a journey which I too may have to go."

Socrates,
Plato's Dialogues

Using Reminiscence

Engaging people in reminiscence is not usually difficult. However, a little preparation will go a long way towards making the experience so much richer. As already stated, reminiscence is a two step process—encouraging memories and listening to them being told. The ability to take a real and genuine interest in people's life stories is what binds the two.

Step 1: Encouraging Memories

Ask leading questions that will help evoke memories. The questions must be relevant to the older adult and her times and so it is important that you familiarize yourself with both. For family members and friends, this foundation has already been laid. Others should find out as much as possible about the individual's past, through family, friends, or anyone who can help give some insight into her personal history, work, hobbies, abilities, likes and dislikes.

Using this information you can formulate questions to stimulate reminiscence:—

"What was it like growing up on a farm?"

"How did you travel to school?"

"Why did you decide to become a musician?"

In the following chapters you will find themes, topics, memory makers and activities which can form the basis for a reminiscence session. Cue questions are also listed which you can use, or customize to suit your situation. Use these guidelines when planning questions:

- Avoid questions which may draw monosyllabic answers.

- Phrase your questions clearly and sensitively.

- Ensure the questions are relevant.

- Look to past skills and achievements for leading questions.

Step 2: Listening To Memories

Because one memory sets off another, reminiscence is seldom linear, and rarely is it an objective, exact image of past events. What is important is the *process* and the feelings invoked. To build a caring relationship with the reminiscer you must be able to listen emphatically and be non-judgmental. Use the following guidelines.

- Be attentive. Interrupt only to ask follow-up questions or when you have a comment which will further the conversation or the speakers line of thinking.

- Show that you are listening and interested through attentive body posture, facial expressions, unhurried tone of voice and maintenance of eye contact.

- Be patient and supportive as memories can sometimes be repetitious and diffuse. Focusing questions on the feelings behind the memory helps.

- Memories evoke a wide range of emotions, sad ones as well as happy ones. Allow the emotions to run their course: tears can be healing. If someone becomes unduly sad and depressed, try to focus on more positive memories and ask uplifting questions about happy events.

- Humor has therapeutic value and it is worthwhile to encourage funny experiences while reminiscing.

- Be aware of the individual's attention span. When he show signs of fatigue or disinterest, wind up the session.

- As you enter and share the older person's world, remember they are trusting you with a part of themselves. Try to comprehend and honor this gift. Thank them for sharing it with you and keep it confidential.

Special Issues

Linking Past And Present

While reminiscing is a powerful tool, its focus should not be limited to the past. Be open to what people are experiencing now. From time to time draw the individual back to the present, using cue questions to connect past and present. This type of discussion strengthens bonds between then and now and preserves a sense of continuity. Talk about how things have changed, for example:

"In what year did you buy this house Mr. Woods?"
"Did you ever think prices would soar so much in your lifetime?"

Concentrate on the present when you draw the session to a close and express your anticipation for meeting again. The focus on both the past, present and future fosters a spirit of hope and anticipation, rather than leaving people open for sad or depressing thoughts.

Reminiscence And Ethnic Heritage

Reminiscence can be used to promote awareness of cultural heritage and transmit the past into history. The ethnic identity of many older adults has been ignored or forgotten. In many instances, they have been so involved in establishing themselves here that their ethnic heritage has not been passed on. In later life, reminiscence can help them to recover this part of themselves, and to share and transmit family history and cultural heritage to younger generations. This strengthens family identity and enables the older person to pass on his unique legacy.

Topics relating to special ethnic skills and interests can be developed for people of different ethnic backgrounds. Listening to their native music or language is a good way to help foreign-born persons recall early events.

Reminiscing With The Alzheimer's Victim

In Alzheimer's disease, memories of the past usually remain much clearer than memories of recent events. It is not surprising that reminiscing can have profound value, especially in the early stages of the disease. Through it, the Alzheimer's victim can be put in touch with a more integrated self. Few activities have as calming an effect on demented patients as speaking about pleasant experiences from the past. By focusing on this remaining skill and using suitable cues and prompts, you can bolster the individual's feeling of self-worth. Reminiscing also enables the person with Alzheimer's to find temporary relief from the harsh reality of their present situation through recalling a more pleasant time.

As an extra benefit, the process of remembering seems to stimulate memory function and may help the mind remain active for longer periods of time.

Following are guidelines for reminiscing with the A.D. victim:

- Reminiscing on a one-to-one basis is the most suitable. Group activities are usually too taxing.

- Always use a focus for the conversation. People with Alzheimer's have difficulty remembering information for more than a few seconds. A relevant memory prop such as a photo, memento or souvenir will help them stay on track.

- Provide stimuli to promote silent reminiscing. Many Alzheimer patients who find it difficult to communicate with others will engage in private reflection. The availability of stimuli such as wall posters, photos and old-time music will facilitate private reminiscence.

- Pitch questions at a level within the person's grasp. It is easy to over stimulate or place excessive demands on the Alzheimer patient's abilities.

- Your expressions and voice tone are as important as the questions you ask. People with Alzheimer's disease have been found to be very sensitive to non-verbal language.

- Go slowly. Allow the person time to absorb questions or stimulus materials. Give her time to respond in whatever way she is able and don't expect dramatic responses or improvements.

Reminiscence In Action

Using the preceeding guidelines, and drawing topics and ideas from the next section of this book, you are ready to begin reminiscing with the older adult.

If possible suggest your visit take place in a quiet, private area away from disturbances. Remember to address the person by their appropriate title—Mr., Mrs., or Miss. Relax and enjoy the adventure of personal involvement which reminiscence brings.

During the visit take note of recurring themes or stories and names which seem important to the individual. Also take note of personal items like photos, old jewelry, memorabilia and souvenirs which might spark memories. When your meeting comes to an end, thank the person for sharing with you and arrange for the next visit. If the situation permits, keep your visits on a weekly basis, bi-weekly at the very least.

In the meantime review your visit and note possible cues for future reminiscence sessions. You will find plenty of material and resources in the following sections to make these sessions enjoyable and successful for everyone.

As your relationship develops, you may like to introduce simple reminiscence activities into your meetings. The second section of this book describes a number of special activities which will add variety to your sessions.

"They are continually talking of the past because they enjoy remembering."

Aristotle,
Rhetoric

Themes for Reminiscence

It's useful to have a bank of reminiscence themes at the ready when you visit an older adult. This section describes various topics from the old days that are designed to get people reminiscing. Sample cue questions are included to get you started. Concentrate on finding a good safe starting point such as *"Favorite Places I've been to"* or *"My best job"* and avoid themes which may cause distress or embarrassment. A sensitive approach is what is called for and soon, people will suggest their own interests, often surprising you with their range of ideas.

Memory Makers such as photographs and books can also be used to generate memories and these are described in detail at the end of Section 1. Sensory aids such as flowers and food can also be used to reinforce the discussion topic and are especially useful if things are slow in getting off the ground.

Guidelines For Choosing And Using Themes

- Use familiar themes to which people can relate. Your profile of the individual will guide you here.

- If a topic seems uncomfortable or stressful to the reminiscer, change it. Keep several topics in reserve.

- Be aware that the *process* is more important than the theme. It's through the *process* of being gently led through the past that the older adult can tap key memories and find them healing.

- Do not span too large a topic at any one session.

- All themes will bring about emotions. Use cue questions and comments to focus on these emotions:
  "How did you feel when that happened?"
  "That must have made you happy!"

- If the reminiscer looks like she wants to say something and is having trouble, be encouraging and supportive:
  "It must be hard to talk about your husband's death."

- Be a good listener.

Cue Questions

Compile a list of cue questions to help you explore each topic. Following each of the following themes is a sample questions list that might be used to stir relevant memories. Cue questions should be regarded as a guide to help you get the discussion going rather than a questionnaire to be followed rigorously. They are helpful in getting the conversation started and in picking up on a particular angle if the conversation lags.

Childhood

Childhood memories linger with us for life and often are our happiest. A myriad of topics can be explored here—schooldays, childhood games and early memories of parents and family.

To stir memories of childhood pastimes, use props such as a kite, yo-yo, marbles, jacks, jump rope and steam engine. Show pictures of these objects, or if you have the item in question, all the better. Compare the simple pastimes of old with today's.

Here are some sample cue questions.

Tell me about your school days

Who was your best friend?

What kinds of things were you interested in as a child?

What did you want to be when you grew up? Why?

Did you have chores and responsibilities at home?

How did you spend summer vacations as a child?

What were some happy pastimes ?

Did you skate, ride horseback, swim?

Do you remember playing hopscotch, hide and seek, marble
  games, spin the top, jump the rope?

What did you enjoy doing during your teenage or later years.

What pastimes do you enjoy now?

Family Life

Reminiscing about family life makes an interesting activity. Using photograph albums, help piece together the individual's family history. Talk about ethnic heritage, family traditions and how holidays were celebrated. Pictures of the person when young can be compared with ones taken as they are now. The development of her own children into adults can be seen.

Reminiscing about family life will evoke varied emotions — be ready for these.

At what age did you have your first child?

How did you decide on the name?

How did you adjust to motherhood?

Have you ever read Dr. Spock on raising children?

Did any of your children resemble you?

Tell me a favorite story about a child in your family

What were some of the difficulties of family life?

What kinds of things did you do together?

Did you have a favorite family member?

What family do you have now?

Have you ever done your family tree?

Have you any special family heirlooms?

On The Farm

Many of today's older adults grew up in rural communities and spent their young days working or helping with farm chores. Their sweetest and fondest memories are often of the simple things they did in those days. They can provide fascinating reminiscences and a treasure of forgotten ways. This may be a good session to record on audio or video cassette, since it will be an oral history of farm life.

Talking about the old days on the farm is an ideal intergenerational activity. The following questions can be used to get the memory juices flowing:

What kinds of chores did you do on the farm?

Did you help with the milking or feed the chickens?

Did you ever work in the onion fields? Did you use a wheelhoe to cultivate them?

What was winter like?

Describe some of the sounds and smells on the farm.

How has dairy farming changed since that time?

Did you ever farm with horses?

Do you recall their names?

Do you remember the early tractors?

What were the advantages of growing up on a farm?

Fashion

Fashion is always a popular subject and can lead to great reminiscences. Get people to talk about their favorite fashions and how styles have changed over the years. Look for pictures which show how fashions have changed down through the decades, get color ads of today's fashions and make comparisons of "then and now."

Here are some cue questions.

Were you fashion-conscious?

What type of clothes did you like to wear?

Did you have a choice or did you wear hand-me-downs?

Do you recall the Gibson Girl look?

When was it in vogue?

Did you ever get your hair bobbed?

What effect did the wars have on fashions?

Was there as much material available then?

When did women start to wear pants?

Have you ever worn knickerbockers?

What kinds of coats did fashionable men wear in the 20's?

What shoes were popular for women in the 30's?

Driving

People will delight in reminiscing about all the cars they remember owning or driving. They can share what it cost to buy and run a car in the old days compared with nowadays and what it was like to ride in the early models.

Do you recall the first time you rode in an automobile?

Tell me about the first trip you took

Do you recall the days when cars only came in black?

Did you learn to drive? Who taught you?

What was the most difficult thing about being a driver?

What kind was your first car? How much did it cost?

What other cars do you recall owning?

What was the speed limit in those days?

How much did gasoline cost then?

Were you ever in a car accident?

Favorite Places

All of us have experienced places that remain in our memories as "favorite places." Many people vividly recall their very first vacation spot right down to the details of how they travelled and where they slept.

For some, a favorite place may be as simple as an old attic, a wood or a special house that lingers on in memory, connecting them to what may at times seem like another world. Reminiscing gives us an opportunity to "go back" to these favorite places of the past.

Tell me a story about your favorite place

Do you have more than one?

Why do you think you remember these places so vividly?

Are there smells or sounds you associate with that place?

How have your favorite places influenced your life?

Do you still return to any of these places?

Have they changed now?

If you could go back there for a visit, what would you do?

Tell me about your most memorable vacation

How did you travel there?

Can you share any mementoes you brought back?

Friends

Friendship is a source of joy throughout life and remembering special friends puts people back in touch with that happiness. People like to talk about friends from different periods: childhood, young adulthood, middle age and the present. The discussion really comes to life if there are photos of old friends to share.

Here are some cue questions:

Do you recall the names of childhood friends?

Are any of them still your friends?

Tell an amusing story about a friend

Who was your best friend ever? Why?

Did you ever have a pen pal?

What are your most treasured memories of friendship?

What kind of people did you choose as friends?

What role did you play: listener, problem-solver?

What kinds of things did you do together?

How long have you known your oldest friend?

Describe this person.

Love And Marriage

Love and courtship are among the most precious of experiences and recalling these can help rekindle some of those feelings. Talk about weddings: white weddings, registry office weddings, famous weddings and royal weddings. Talk about changing trends in marriage—younger marriages and people having more than one marriage. Bring the topic to life with old wedding albums and props such as rings, posies, invitations cards and telegrams.

Tell me about your first romance, your first dance or date.

Do you recall writing and receiving many love letters?

What were Valentine days like long ago?

How and where did you meet your husband, wife?

What activities and places did you enjoy while dating?

Who proposed? Describe what happened.

Work Life

As anyone knows who has worked with elderly people, the value of work and the pride in one's occupations is very evident. This is particularly the case with persons who have no children and whose main source of personal satisfaction came through their work role. A discussion built around this subject prompts sharing of experiences and feelings of accomplishment.

Using picture cards illustrating particular jobs, ask people what they did for a living and why they chose that particular job. Many people have unfulfilled desires concerning the life's work they hoped for; they had to change plans due to money problems, early marriage, a death in the family or other unanticipated events. Find out about these "paths not taken" and the feelings surrounding them.

Tell me about your first job

Do you recall how you spent your first paycheck?

When did you begin working full-time?

How did you get the job?

Was there any special training involved?

Did you feel that you had a special calling to this work?

31

Old Remedies

Natural home remedies were commonplace long ago, much more so than a trip to the doctor. Nearly all the cookery books of old had a section on Remedies. In the absence of doctors, nurses and hospitals, every mother had a supply of home remedies for every type of ailment.

Every family had its favorites: flax-seed tea to relive coughs, peppermint oil for colic, browned flour for diaper rash, goose grease for a cold, honey in hot lemon tea for a cough. Warm oil was applied to inner-ear infections and cloves eased the pain of toothache. Hot compresses were used for boils, while Epsom salts, baking soda or vinegar were applied to mosquito bites and other stings.

Many beauty concoctions were used such as lemon juice to brighten the hair, cooked flaxseed for hairsetting gel and mashed cucumbers for a face mask.

In today's world of antibiotics and miracle cures, we are skeptical of these old-fashioned cures; the young hardly know they existed.

Here are some cue questions to help bring this colorful and sometimes amusing aspect of the past to life again:

What are your memories of being sick as a child?

Do your recall any remedies your mother used?
  Tell us about them

Do you remember eating sugar to cure hiccups?

Did your mother ever use cobwebs to stop bleeding?

Did you ever treat a cold with goose grease rubs
  Did it work?

Did you ever soak an injury in hot water and Epsom
  salts, cover with fat meat and wrap?

When you stepped on a nail, did you soak your foot in
  water with ashes from the wood stove?

Do you remember having hot cider vinegar and salt
  poured over a sprained ankle?

Was warm smoke from an old clay pipe ever blown
  into your ear to cure an earache?

Did your mother ever rub fat on warts to cure them?

What tonics were popular?

Did your family doctor make housecalls?

Did you go to the doctor or did you try remedies first?

Did you ever see a medicine show?
  What was it like? Did you buy any remedies at it?

Superstitions

Superstitions were part and parcel of everyday life long ago. Many parts of the country had different superstitions, some of which came from the Old World with the immigrants. Here are some cue questions and tidbits to help evoke memories of this old lore.

Were you ever superstitious?

Are people more or less superstitious nowadays?

Tell me some of the superstitions you grew up with.

Have you ever been afraid to walk under a ladder?

Did you know anyone born on Friday the 13th?

Have you ever been lucky or unlucky on this date?

Did you or your parents have any special good luck charms?

Did you ever carry a rabbit's foot, a buckeye or a clover?

Did you ever break the wishbone of a turkey?

Have you ever thrown a pinch of salt over your left shoulder?

Popular Superstitions

Here are some superstitions that were popular in earlier times. Many more will surface during the course of the discussion.

An itching elbow means you will be sleeping in a strange bed shortly.

A lock of hair is a good luck charm.

A hairy chest is a sign of strength and luck in life.

Hairy arms indicate wealth.

An itchy right palm means money or good news is on the way.

An itchy left palm means you will spend money soon.

Never cut your hair when the moon is waning; if you do it will thin and fall out.

The Decades

The decades, each equally rich, distinct and colorful, make a lively topic for exploring. Memories peculiar to each one come flooding back with prompting —memories of entertainment, advertising, work, leisure, home life and transport, to name but a few.

Postcards and photographs set the scene for personal reminiscence and create the opportunity for sharing these memories with others. Combined with music, radio, books and other memory makers, past decades spring vividly to mind.

The 1920's

They were called the Roaring Twenties. The unique speed and rhythm of this era was tempered by a lifestyle, morality and excitement unknown to other decades. The twenties bring back memories of the jazz age. Women bobbed their hair, wore short skirts and went to dance-a-thons that sometimes lasted for days. Hip flasks and speak-easies became commonplace with the advent of Prohibition. This was both a prosperous and fun time and one which today's elders will recall like no other. Using pictures of the famous faces and dances of that age, you can help elicit a treasure trove of memories.

Here are some memory rousers from the world of fashion, entertainment, advertising and politics:

Why was this called the Jazz Age?
Did you wear raccoon coats or turned down hose?
Which fashions were the most outrageous? The most popular? Your favorite?
Did you read the popular magazines **Good House**

keeping *and* **Ladies Home Journal**?

Do you recall the **Ziegfeld Follies**?

Did you go to vaudeville?

What do you remember about flappers?

What was the mood when Lindbergh completed his flight to Paris?

Do you recall the Burma Shave signs?

How did you feel when women won the right to vote?

How did Prohibition affect your life?

What was your reaction to the Stockmarket crash?

Do you recall much about Al Capone?

What do you remember about the Ku Klux Klan?

Do you remember Duke Ellington? Babe Ruth?

The 1930's

Many of today's elders have vivid memories of the Great Depression which followed the euphoria of the 20's. They can recall the stark realities of bread lines, unemployment lines, bank closings and dust storms. Yet these years which were full of tragedy and despair were equally rich in culture. This duality will probably be reflected in peoples' reminiscences.

Describe your memories of The Depression.

What did people use instead of money?

What did many men start selling on street corners?

How did families deal with hunger?

Did you have friends who migrated to California in the 30's ?

Do you recall the bread lines; unemployment lines?

What were the dust storms like?

Tell me about the popular pastimes — card playing, miniature golf, jigsaw puzzles.

The 1940's

Reminisce with people about daily life during the war. Find out how their lives were affected by rationing, munition factories, evacuation and conscription. Look at the tragic and humorous events of the war, both local and abroad.

Use all the memory aids you can find—ration books, identity cards, gas masks, medals, music, wartime cook books, newspaper cuttings. Use pictures of life during the war, pictures of women at work, fire watching and friends who were lost in action. All will facilitate excursions into the past. These questions can serve as a guide.

How old were you when the war started?

Where did you live?

Did you have to wait in line to get everything?

Who did the waiting in your family?

What was the hardest rationed item to adjust to?

How did people stretch the rations?

Did you keep a Victory Garden?

What was the role of women during the war?

What sort of entertainment was popular during the war?

What radio programs did you enjoy during the forties?

Who were the big names in sport then?

What was happening in Hollywood during the forties?

Do you remember Liz Taylor in the early days?

"A picture speaks a thousand words."

Anon

Memory Makers

Recollections of the past spring more readily and vividly to mind through the use of memory makers. Personal objects and documents, music, photographs, poems and recipes from yesteryear can unearth a treasure-trove of memories. They take the older adult back in time and a vivid reverie begins.

Equally evocative items might include an early driver's licence, high school year book, birth and death certificates and titles of home ownership. Family artifacts, heirlooms and souvenirs are also invaluable memory makers.

Jewelry can stir memories and most people will have a ring or necklace with special significance. Family members may have access to old diaries and letters; these will help to stir memories of important life events.

These kinds of articles, many which have lain in basements for years unused and unnoticed, take on a new importance as they are used for reminiscence. Each has its own significance and often holds different meanings for other family members.

An atlas might be useful to point out where the person has come from. Old maps can be used to pin-point corner-stones and routes within the community. Old price lists can provoke interesting comments about how times have changed.

Nothing prompts recall like photographs. Pictures of family vacations can spark off tales of summer vacations through the years. Pictures of the cars older adults have owned bring back fond memories of time and place. Pictures of movie stars, entertainers, politicians or other famous and familiar faces from the old days are a powerful jogger of memories. Even very old photos of local places are of interest because people can talk about changes they have witnessed locally within their lifetime. Organizing photos by themes such as holidays, vacations, residences, employment, friendships, weddings or any number of other topics turns photo albums and old address books into powerful resources.

Old books provide excellent trigger materials. History books which show pictures of the war years, the Depression and other events provide an evocative browsing source. Likewise, old recipe books are potentially a rich source of discussion ideas. Fashion books and magazines produce fascinating reminiscences and comparisons with current fashions produce interesting comments. Early issues of magazines like *Ladies Home Journal* or *Mc Call's* are particularly interesting to women, as are pattern books which can be obtained from fabric stores at reasonable prices.

Old catalogs from Sears and Montgomery Ward provide pictures of many everyday items with which older adults were familiar. These serve as visual reminders of the types of products being advertised in olden times, and contrasted with their contemporary versions, these will provoke many memories.

Books from childhood resonate strongly with older people. Old school books like *McGuffey's Eclectic Reader*s will bring back many memories. Many of these have been reprinted and are now available in bookstores and libraries. "Then and Now" books provide pictorial accounts of how places and things have changed over the years and there are now some interesting varieties available.

Back issues of *Look* or *Life* magazines provide pictures and stories about film stars, singers, celebrities and politicians. Many other magazines are rich sources of old advertisements which are good discussion starters. You can cut these out, mount and display them.

Also, back issues of local and national newspapers are helpful in building up a picture of the times and in generating ideas for discussion. Many newspapers now have a regular column that features news of the day from 10 and 25 years ago. These news items are well worth collecting and saving as they can produce vivid recollections. Certain columnists that date way back (such as *"Dear Abby"* and *"Ann Landers"*) are also worth cutting out. They provoke lively discussions and shed light on changing attitudes to morality and customs.

Postcards stimulate happy memories as they have strong associations with holidays, friends, family and lovers. They form excellent stimulus material for a wide range of project work and discussion groups.

Use a variety of trigger materials to stimulate all the senses. The texture and smell of an object are just as important as what it looks like. Some people are visual—photos will bring back memories. For others, it's the music. Still others need something to pick up and touch or smell. So it's important to use multi-sensory stimulus materials.

Our senses have a way of keeping our pasts alive. For some, the tasting of food can bring back happy memories of cooking. Foods can remind us of holidays past: for example, turkey and pumpkin pie remind us of Thanksgiving, cookies and baked treats of Christmas and candy of Easter. And there are foods associated with the seasons of the year as well as with special occasions. These foods themselves take on heavy emotional significance.

Textures and shapes of all kinds may be included in your stock of memory makers. The sense of touch is a major line of communication and there are myriads of different consistencies and shapes—old tools or clothing— any one of which might conjure up a happy past or, conversely, a sad event.

As for aromas, evocative scents can range from food and spices to flowers, potpourri, tobacco, and perfume. The French writer Marcel Proust based one of his most famous literary passages on a moment in which the narrator experiences a flood of childhood memories simply by smelling a familiar pastry. Bring in objects to produce visual *and* olfactory stimulation.

Outside smells are very gratifying, especially if one has been inside for months. The outside world with its smells of earth, fresh rain, perfume and mown grass can be very healing. The smells of nature can bring a whole flood of memories and can be helpful in extending the concentration period. There is really no limit to what might be used to spark familiarity or contrast.

How To Use Memory Makers

Make sure that older adults have the best possible opportunity of relating to the memory makers. Try to compensate for sensory handicaps. Visually impaired people, for example, can be exposed to musical materials (rather than books or photographs) and objects which capitalize on touch and smell. Anything that has specific tactile associations will help the recollection process. It is also important that the memory makers are presented in such a way that the person is not overwhelmed. Know the individual's capabilities.

It is extremely important that the material presented be relevant to the individual's past experiences. With a person who has lived and worked on a farm all their life, you may find that books, illustrations and models of farm animals bring back memories of pleasant, productive, useful times in life. Show pictures relevant to the planting, cultivation and harvesting of crops and invite her to 'feel' and describe the relevant objects to stimulate sensory perception. Former teachers may respond to pictures related to school days and housewives to ingredients and kitchen utensils. If a person was once a carpenter, old woodworking magazines will spark memories of the trade, the smell of wood, the rasp of the saw.

A show and tell approach (as children do in school) is a good way to get people talking about memory makers. Photos or pictures of early model cars, a beautiful quilt, old film posters, historic events, old toys and steamships if any were immigrants (or children of immigrants) are some universal topics of interest.

You can set up a collection of folders for each topic. Pictures can be cut from magazines, categorized into themes and be accompanied by a list of questions. These are a great help for getting a conversation started off or for picking it up if it lags and are a real asset especially when one is a novice to reminiscing.

Where To Find Memory Makers

Finding appropriate memory joggers is not difficult. As ideas take shape, articles will simply accumulate. Family members and friends will have more resources of a personal nature available to them. Others should talk to the family or the older person and find out what photos, objects and ephemera they might have. Be sensitive: these are often the person's most treasured possessions.

Much rich material can evolve from the resources in your community—the library, historical society, businesses. Contact your local history center. They will be able to advise where to obtain copies of photographs, newspaper articles and other raw materials. Music libraries may also be helpful. Look for sing-a-long recordings and music of the big band era.

You will find many varieties of ethnic music here too. Some libraries have slide tapes, combining pictures, sounds and music from the past, and if these are suitable to your situation, use them. The main library will often have a local history department which may contain a collection of photographs and documents. They may also have addresses of local history societies which may be able to help in the gathering of material and making of useful contacts. Some libraries hold periodic sales of old books and sometimes you can be lucky enough to come across vintage material for reminiscence here.

The person's former place of employment may have photographs of the work place and the work force. They may allow you to copy these and may even help you compile a collection of a particular trade's tools.

Other sources for stimulating props are used book or record stores. You may be able to find rare 'nostalgia' and comic books there as well as a good variety of Americana, posters, records, sheet music, and catalogs. Estate and yard sales are especially good for nostalgic objects. Be on the lookout for bits of old ephemera from attics or cupboards—flat irons, washboards, gas masks, old magazines and forgotten childhood collections of postcards and cigarette cards are some of the treasures which may be found there. Search thrift stores and stores that sell vintage clothing.

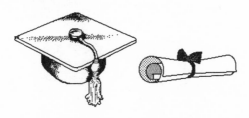

Local photographic societies may be able to offer their skills and resources in copying old photographs— either as slides or as prints. Specialist libraries and archives may also prove useful. Some museums and libraries publish old photographs as postcard sets which may be purchased quite cheaply.

Many local museums have collections of everyday objects from early twentieth century homes, and occasionally they lend these to schools. See if they are willing to lend some small objects to you for reminiscence. Some museums and libraries may set up an old time exibition for senior centers, church groups or nursing homes. If the situation permits, you might bring the older person to the exhibition to explore things at their leisure. They will enjoy fingering through highly evocative items which were a vital part of their growing up. Items such as old irons, candlesticks, sewing machines, kitchen utensils, farm tools, toys and cooking stoves will bring back many good memories. If you can photograph these items, or at least make a list of them, you will have the makings of a stimulating reminiscence discussion afterwards.

Your very best resources are the people you know or

meet. People in your community have family albums, attics, ideas, stories and skills to share. Just let your friends and neighbors know what you're looking for and you will be surprised by the range of memory makers that come your way.

*"When you truly possess all you have
been and done, which may take some time,
you are fierce with reality."*

Florida Scott-Maxwell, 1968

Reminiscing through Activities

This section describes simple activities which stimulate reminiscence. Activities are an effective, easy and enjoyable way of uncovering memories, drawing from them and of adding variety to reminiscence sessions.

The activities described in the following pages are failure-free and among others include arts and crafts, music, reading and intergenerational reminiscing. Most can be completed in one session or carried out over a few.

Keep in mind the following guidelines when planning and using the reminiscence activities in this section.

- Take the older adult's personal profile into consideration when selecting activities and remember that some activities will be more suitable than others.

- Gear reminiscence activities to correspond with the individual's current state of awareness and comprehension. Avoid activities which you think might frustrate, confuse or threaten the individual's sense of competence.

- Never force an activity on someone. Accept that it may take some time and gently introduce the activity again later.

- Be alert to how each activity affects the individual. The most successful activities are those which evoke pleasant associations from the past and touch on old, familiar joys.

- Be calm and unhurried in your approach and give people ample time to respond.

"The mind never photographs, it paints pictures."

Pear, 1927

Arts
and
Crafts

Memory is the seed of much creativity. In Greek mythology, Mnemosyne, the goddess of memory, is mother of the muses. Naturally, Arts and Crafts are wonderful channels for expressing memories!

Because scenes and colors provoke associations and memories, people often reminiscence spontaneously while painting or drawing. For those who can no longer communicate verbally, art may be one of the most effective modalities for self-expression. The senses of touch and sight are stimulated as well as memory.

Sketching Memories

Encourage people to sketch scenes of their memories. They can picture in their mind a scene that was particularly enjoyable or that had special meaning. Memories of events, people or places from their childhood can be both happy and sad.

Capturing images on paper seems to bring back long-forgotten details and to make more vivid the pictures. This is particularly true in the case of depressed or confused individuals. These details often provide wonderful cues for reminiscence discussion.

A Family Portrait

Ask the individual to sketch her family portrait. You might suggest that she arrange people in positions that symbolize their position in the family. Encourage her to talk about the picture. Here are some cue questions to get people started:

Who is in the center of the picture?

Where are you in the picture?

Does anyone seem to be left out?

Is anyone touching?

What's the mood of the picture?

Childhood Bedroom

This scene can evoke many memories. Here are some cue questions to help older adults visualize their childhood bedroom.

Did you share your room with anyone?

What did you like most about your room?

What was it like? How big was it?

Can you draw a picture of it or a floor plan?

Was it warm and comfortable?

Schooldays

Memories of schooldays stay with us all through life. A sketch of the old classroom will bring back a flood of memories, details and stories about teachers and friends. The following cues should get the memories flowing.

See if you can close your eyes and pretend you're back

in your first classroom:

What does it feel like? Is it crowded?

Describe your feelings about being in your room.

What are the sounds? The smells?

What are the colors? The important objects?

Painting To Music

Play recordings of soothing classical music and have the individual move his paint brush to the music. You might have to initiate the activity at first. If he likes to listen to old tunes, play a recording and discuss what the story is about.

Suggest that he work with the paint to make a picture, design or pattern related to the story or to the mood of the music. Water colors are best for this kind of activity.

Coloring

Coloring is a peaceful activity and there are many varieties of adult coloring books available. Look for coloring books with pictures of objects of days gone by like brass beds, wood burning stoves, classic automobiles, crank telephones.

Coloring books which emphasize nature are also useful for reminiscence. Coloring and discussing the images such such as herbs, flowers, trees, seasore life, all help stimulate memories.

Bear in mind these guidelines when doing art-work.

- The work does not have to be aesthetically pleasing and there are no rights or wrongs. It's simply a way of communicating ideas and memories through line and color.

- As in all other activities, use only non-toxic adult art materials. Some older adults may need special assistance and the activities should be supervised. Always present the activity as appropriate for adults.

REMINISCING THROUGH CRAFT WORK

Family members can reminisce with relatives about the crafts of old. They can tell the significance old-fashioned crafts and activities had for them, and where possible, they can teach and demonstrate some of these skills.

Older adults who were raised on farms often have clear memories of many crafts now almost obsolete. They can demonstrate these by sketches or photos as they describe the procedure. In buttermaking, for example, they might draw the butter churns, butter molds and butter paddle.

56

Quilt making is another art at which many elders were adept. By relating quilting memories and experiences, the older individual will be put in touch with a vital part of the past and gain a sense of their own competence and skills. This type of demonstration will also give you a chance to learn about an old-fashioned craft that has become a modern form of art and self-expression.

Other crafts can be demonstrated such as needlepoint, basket making, drying flowers—anything in fact, which pertains to skills learned long ago.

Collages

Pictures remind us of significant events or important people in our lives. A wall-sized collage can tell a story in a much more interesting way than a rambling spoken account.

Making A Collage

Collages are easy to make. First select a theme for the collage. Then encourage the older adult to look through magazines and catalogs and cut out pictures that strike a chord. Help him to glue or paste them in place.

Life Collages

If the person lacks the coordination and dexterity to cut out the shapes himself, then do it for him. Make sure that the shapes to be cut out are simple and fairly large. The following are good themes for collages.

Life Collages

A life collage is a wonderful medium for releasing memories. The contents should include: a short written biographical sketch mentioning former occupation, achievements and interests; photos of family and friends and pictures of places lived in.

An additional benefit of making a life collage is that the process increases self-esteem. It helps people recognize just how much they've done, how far they've grown, and all they've accomplished in their lives. The written proof is right in front of them!

State Collage

A map of the state in which the individual grew up can be created in the form of a collage. The process is simple: once an outline of the state is drawn or cut out, it is pasted onto poster-board. Some of the things manufactured, grown, or marketed there may be pasted in. Add any other things that state is famous for.

Nature Collage

Have people look through magazines and catalogs and cut out pictures of wildlife. Or, they can collect real objects from nature such as twig leaves, moss and pine cones and paste them on to poster-board to make a collage. This kind of project can lead to soothing and enjoyable reminiscences about time spent in nature—boating, camping and fishing.

Discussion can occur during and after the activity.

What does the collage mean to you?

Does it bring back memories? What kind?

What is the feeling of the pictures?

What do you like best about this collage?

What will you do with it?

"It is to live twice when we can enjoy recollections of our former life."

Martial

Did You Ever?

For a lively reminiscing session, select from magazines pictures of scenes which will stir memories. Make sure they are large, clear and colorful. Cut and mount them on uniform size cardboard.

On the back of each card put comments about the picture and a series of simple, straightforward questions. Books such as *IDEALS* are excellent sources of pictures. Show a picture and ask the question: *Did You Ever...?* Complete the question with such statements as....*move house?....have a bar-be-cue?...eat Chinese food?* Once the subject has been covered, select a new picture and begin again.

Here are some examples of what to include:

Did You Ever—

visit an art gallery	*sit in a hot spring*
visit a court session	*see a lion*
go to a beach	*see a shooting star*

Did you ever cook over an open fire?

Did you ever:

go to a flea market

go berry picking

see a circus

take a cruise

stay on a farm

go backpacking

sleep in a cabin

sleep in a tent

act in a play

have a house burglarized

take part in a cattle drive

have a pet

bake bread

play an instrument

move house

go swimming

have a bar-be-cue

go to a wake

Did you ever go canoeing?

61

"...Memories refresh and elevate the soul and are a source of my best enjoyment."

Tolstoy,
Childhood, Boyhood and Youth

Games

For many people, trading anecdotes is a popular social activity. However some individuals may be too shy or confused for such impromptu reminiscing.

Games provide these individuals with an opportunity to reminisce in a more structured setting. There are many board games available which help evoke the past and provide cognitive stimulation as well as entertainment. When using these games, clear the table of anything which might be distracting. Table-tops which are pattern-free, smooth and not shiny are best for confused persons who are easily distracted. If the table top has a design, cover it with a cloth of a single, solid color. Square tables give the most versatility in arrangement patterns.

Penny Ante

This is a non-demanding and entertaining card game reminiscent of poker. Designed to gently stimulate memory, each card instructs the player to give or take a penny based on remembering a certain event.

Reminiscence Bingo

Reminiscence bingo is useful in promoting interaction and in encouraging life review. The playing cards are arranged in squares of five across and consist of pictures of old objects related to the past such as tools, kitchen items, clothing styles and automobiles. Pictures may be cut from magazines or catalogs or they may be drawn in by hand. The old reprinted Sears catalogs have many useful varieties. The game is played much like regular bingo; items are called out by name and players match them accordingly. Alternatively, pictures may be shown to allow the players to visually match the objects.

Reminiscence Jigsaws

Jigsaws make for an interesting and stimulating activity when the subject is of interest to the older person. Try to find suitable themes to do with the past — old modes of transportation, boats, cars, trains etc. These, along with childhood scenes, old houses and objects, can be used as springboards to discussing the past.

Simple puzzles with an uncomplicated design and a limited number of large pieces work best. More complex puzzles can be used if the person is just required to get in the last four or five pieces rather than do it from start to finish.

Three Score And Ten,

This board game is designed to spark lively conversation in those over 50. The game is played by two to seven players on a seven-sided rainbow board. It creates a social, competitive climate for reminiscing through mix and match cards which focus on memories and feelings about places, items, times and events of the past.

Seven sets of mix and match cards lie in a plastic tray at the board's center. Players roll dice to move pawns around the board. When a pawn reaches the board's center, a card is turned over to reveal an instruction such as *"Recite a story."*

As other pawns arrive at the board's center, more cards are turned face up until a complete sentence forms. For example, a sentence may read, "Person to the right should recite two funny childhood memories or three embarrassing events."

Each deck contains 10 cards, providing numerous sentence combinations. Other topics include special meals or old-fashioned social customs. Playing time can last anywhere from 30 minutes to hours.

Generations

Generations is a family reminiscence game designed to be played by members from two or more generations, ie. adult children with aging parents or teenagers with middle-aged parents. A series of 768 questions about the past allows older people to reminisce in a positive way. Each player has their own game chart and turns a spinner to determine the question to which they respond. Questions are divided into age categories such as birth to 10 years , 10 to 20 years, and questions are also divided into six life areas—career, family, relationships, spiritual life, and leisure. For example, "In the years between 30 and 40 what were the personal goals you were trying to achieve?" Each question is meant to be provocative and helpful in the process of life review.

Cross Country

Cross Country is a colorful board game which provides structured reminiscence for players as they travel across the United States and stop off at well-known cities and tourist attractions along the way. Players move across country by drawing destination cards — each one containing entertaining facts and a bit of history about the location — to see where they'll go next. The object is to see who will be first to get across the country. From the comfort of a favorite armchair, players can share the remembered pleasures of vacations from years gone by. This is also an excellent way for grandparents and grandchildren to spend time together.

Appendix 4 lists the addresses for obtaining the above games.

Other Games

Charades

This is one of the most popular acting/guessing games. Make individual slips for each of the following actions and pass them out to each group member. Ask them to pantomime the action when their turn comes up. These actions stimulate memory-sharing and many can be done in a wheelchair.

doing the waltz

typing

raising a flag up the flagpole

hanging out clothes on clothesline

milking a cow

washing clothes on a washboard

going to the dentist

casting and catching a fish

square dancing

toasting marshmallows over a camp-fire

voting in an election

Crossword Puzzles

1924 was the year of the crossword puzzle and many elderly people will recall having whittled away evenings in their youth completing crossword puzzles with their families. Solving a crossword puzzle of the early kind can make for a nostalgic group activity.

Name The Ad

An interesting activity can be created by naming the slogan for various products and having people guess the product. This game works well with adver tisements from the past, and can lead to some interest ing memories. Following are examples of slogans:

"When it rains, it pours"   (Morton's Salt)

"His master's voice"   *(Victrola)*

"Good to the last drop"   *(Maxwell House Coffee)*

"Makes clothes sparkle"   *(Oxydol)*

*"Isn't each of us struck silent and attentive when we hear an
old man or old woman utter the magic words,
'Now I will tell you the story of my life...'"*

Harry Moody, 1984

The
Life Story

The telling of one's life story makes a wonderful reminiscence activity. Once captured in words and pictures,
the life story makes a valuable social document and is a
true legacy to leave to family and friends. Life stories,
often recorded on video or audio tape and later transcribed onto paper, are known as oral histories.

There is an old African saying which reminds us that
when an old person dies, an entire library is destroyed.
Unless culture and traditions are passed on to other generations the knowledge dies with them. Oral history is
perhaps the best way of preserving the library of local
and family history that otherwise would be lost to future
generations.

**Recording an individual's life story has many advan-
tages:**

- It helps to preserve continuity between generations.
- It offers a sense of how an individual life is part of a
  larger historical and cultural process.

67

- It can lead to a deepened sense of identity, meaning and dignity for the older adult.

- This type of reminiscing gives a real sense of one's interconnectedness with the world.

- Through sharing life stories of pain, comfort, survival and hope, older persons also gain a sense of their own competence and mastery over life events.

- Life histories make one aware of one's roots, one's heritage and one's cultural context.

Encouraging The Individual

Some people are natural raconteurs and relish the opportunity of telling their life story. Others protest that they have nothing of value to say because their lives were ordinary.

Many people need to be convinced of the value of their reminiscences and reassured that people will have an interest in their experiences. Stress the importance of preserving their family history, a history that may not be known to others in their families and therefore would be lost. Emphasize that all the taping (or writing) will be done by the one interviewer in private and that they need only tell the stories with which they are comfortable.

Say something like this:

"Dad, I'd like to hear your life story. Could you tell me about your parents, your early memories and what life was like when you were growing up. I will be using the tape recorder when you speak so that I can make a living record of your memories. This is something special which we will always have and which your great grandchildren can hear."

Once recorded, people can feel quite excited at hearing their memories played back and preserved.

Preparing for the Recording

Even if you're going to record your own mother's and father's life stories, you have to prepare. For example, you have to decide on what areas you are going to cover. Family life? School years? Work life?

Arrange the session well in advance to give the individual a chance to collect and clarify her thoughts.

Memory Makers

Gather materials such as photographs, maps and newspapers — anything that might help to encourage the memories that you want to record. For instance, if you're reminiscing about food during the war, old recipe books and ration books would be ideal. Documents such as passports, citizenship papers or marriage certificates also serve as catalysts in stimulating memories.

Reviewing these together will help the individual remember stories or past experiences which can then be recorded.

The Interview Process

A reminiscence interview is not like a television or radio interview — it should really be like a good conversation, with you, the interviewer taking a back seat. While the interview should be relaxed and free-flowing, it is also organized into large blocks of time or themes: childhood, school, marriage, work, and so on.

Try to help the older person feel relaxed and ensure the recording process is not intimidating. If it goes well, the individual may feel quite excited at hearing his memories played back and preserved.

Asking Questions

Think out the key questions you want to ask to help give an overall structure to the interview. This checklist of questions should be used as a guide, as sparingly and discreetly as possible, just to jog your memory. Use key words, rather than writing out questions in full.

Be aware that the memories an individual selects are influenced by the format and tone of the questions you ask. Stressing one type of question can adversely shape the interview. Closed questions will yield too many 'yes' or 'no' answers while too many open-ended questions can result in an interview which lacks purpose and direction.

Ask questions that will encourage more than 'yes' or 'no' answers. Jot them down so that they progress easily from one event to the next in orderly fashion.

For example: Mrs. K, you were already 30 years old when the Great Depression struck. What type of work were you doing at the time? How did the announcement of the stock market crash affect you? What effect did the Depression have on your family? The community? What are some of the memories you have of that period?

As well as the classic objective questions of who, what, when and where, questions which invite more open-ended and descriptive answers should also be used. Questions which begin with *"Describe..."*, *"Tell me about..."* *"Explain ..."*, *"Expand on.."* *"Compare..."* often trigger more reflective and descriptive anecdotes.

One way to organise the questions is in chronological order — school years, pre-marriage, married years, work years, retirement years and then focus on special experiences, changes, clothing styles, religious concepts, world events, etc during those times.

Ways To Record A Life Story

A life story can be recorded in a number of ways. Whatever medium is selected, it's crucial that all recorded material be shown to the person interviewed and that any public use of it be negotiated with that person. This will prevent misunderstandings. Always tell the person you are taking notes or taping and explain how you plan to use the material.

You may want to consider a brief release form that simply grants you full permission to use the material for educational and historical purposes and is signed by the interviewee.

A Written Story

You may choose to transcribe the story or at least to note down the central aspects. Right after an interview is the best time to type up or write out your notes and transcribe tapes. You may also want to edit the material then — punctuate, paragraph and eliminate irrelevant information.

If you want to take photographs, Foxfire recommends a single-lens reflex camera but you could also use a Polaroid or an Instamatic, depending on how you plan to use the photos. No matter what camera you use, you want clearly focused, story-telling pictures.

Transcribed stories look impressive when they are typed and people will appreciate copies which can be shown to friends and relatives. Seeing their stories in black and white will help bolster self-esteem. By presenting their stories back in written form, they are continually being stimulated to engage in more storytelling.

An Audio Recording

If you have access to a tape recorder, you can tape the individual's life story. Hand-held cassette recorders which can cost as little as $60 are all that many of us can afford. If used carefully and in combination with a microphone of good quality, you can make good recordings.

Always use a separate microphone. Built-in microphones pick up the background hum of the recorder's motor, which can be noticeable and may ruin the recording. Position the micropone correctly to avoid any unwanted noise. For most microphones, a position 6 to 18 inches away from the speaker's mouth is best. Make test recordings with friends or family before recording the biography.

Film And Video

Although memories may be recorded well using audio tapes, they are even more absorbing when the medium is film or video. Here the scope and possibilities are endless. If you haven't got access to a recording system, rent one. Make sure the tapes are of the best possible quality as you want them to last for many years to come.

As the person talks, you can film her as unobtrusively as possible. You might also want to videotape favorite family treasures collected over the years. Do the same with old photos, documents, maps and newspaper clippings which help to illustrate parts of the story.

Where To Make The Recording

Conduct the interview in a quiet comfortable room where the person will feel relaxed and open. Take a recorder into different types of acoustic environments so you can judge for yourself the effects of recording in a yard, on a street corner, or in a room with a noisy refrigerator.

The worst acoustic environment is often found in the kitchen where uncarpeted floors, flat painted walls, appliance noise and a high activity level can result in many audible distractions. While it is tempting to think of the kitchen as homey and therefore a good site for an interview, in reality it may be noisy and inappropriate.

Living rooms, dining rooms and studies provide better acoustics for recording. Carpeted floors, draperies, bookcases and sound absorbing furniture are positive factors. Furthermore these rooms are often outside the mainstream of pedestrian traffic. Special acoustic problems such as ticking or chiming clocks, telephones or even the family pet should be considered.

Special Tips

- Enjoy the process. Don't tire yourself or the interviewee out — a half-hour to one-hour per session is enough.

- Realise that recalling different memories will arouse all kinds of feelings in both of you. Be understanding!

- Don't feel you have to be in total control all the time. Allow people to wander in their reminiscing.

- Don't talk too much and avoid encouraging noises or interrupting with further questions. Show interst in a non-verbal way by nodding or smiling.

- After the interview, don't rush off. People will feel offended if you leave as soon as it is finished. Leave time for a chat and be prepared to talk about yourself too.

"Memory is where the proof of life is stored. It offers material for stock-taking and provides clues about where our lives are going.

Norman Cousins,
The Healing Heart

Life Writing

Many people draw great pleasure from writing about the past and this can be encouraged as a creative reminiscence activity. The writing of memoirs, autobiography, or personal and family history—life writing as it is often called— is currently popular as an individual or group activity for older adults. Many senior centers, community colleges and adult education programs offer classes in life writing.

Writing has many benefits:

- It creates satisfaction in being able to express oneself.

- It allows sharing of meaningful experiences with peers.

- Writing provides an outlet for expressing one's talent.
- It helps preserve life-lore for future generations.

Life History Writing

Writing one's life story is a powerful evoker of the past. As one event is recalled, that memory leads to another, and another, and so on. Through this process of association, the individual can see how one life event is connnected to another, how things are tied together, linked not only in memory but in reality.

Writing a life history provides an individual with the opportunity to answer for her life and to clarify for herself what her life means. People are often surprised to discover the experience and knowledge that their lives contain.

The process can be cathartic, enabling people to release pent-up feelings and to work through old conflicts and griefs from the past. This unloading of emotional baggage is a tremendous relief. It provides an opportunity for individuals to move into the future with renewed energy and fresh purpose.

The writing process helps integrate one's life experiences and promotes self-acceptance, while the sharing process promotes a feeling of closeness to other people.

Family members and friends enjoy reading life histories. They learn from them and see a new dimension of history. Life histories, then, are useful for the people who write them and useful for those who read them.

The Memory Book

The life history may be written in a memory book. Providing a written and pictorial record of the individual's life, the memory book highlights distant memories and gives a means of using these constructively. It can be compiled at a leisurely pace conducive to reminiscing.

There are several ready-to-use varieties of memory books available in bookstores. Alternatively you can make one from a scrapbook. At the top of each page, write headings such as "Earliest Memories," "School Days," "My Best Friend," "Early Ambitions," "Family Life," "My First Job," "My Wedding," "Raising My Family," "Vacations," "Retirement," "The Future."

Family members can become involved, working with the person and slowly piecing together the highlights of his life. Pictures, headlines and news items from old newspapers and magazines can be pasted in where appropriate, to put the person's life in context. The local library or historical society may have additional material which would help to illustrate what was happening locally. If there are children in the family, leafing through the memory book will help them to share something from the older person's past.

The memory book can become a kind of *"This Is Your Life"* album that the individual will find interesting and captivating when alone. In nursing homes and retirement centers, staff members may enjoy seeing it and getting to know the person better.

Facilitating Life History Writing

Life history writing is not about turning out a literary masterpiece. Instead, it involves trying to capture part of the past on paper, in one's own way. Simplicity is the key to successful life writing.

Getting Started

One of the most common barriers in getting started is the fear of the writing process. If this hang-up can be overcome, life writing can be helpful and therapeutic.

One way of freeing people to write is by letting them be aware that there are many options. Don't limit someone to writing straight prose; perhaps she can write a poem instead. Or—the life story may be written in the form of a letter to someone. The bottom line is to write in ways that will best capture one's life the way it's been lived.

Writing Exercise

The writing exercises below are helpful in getting people started writing their life histories.

Cue Questions

The focus here is on knowing how one's life *felt*—what were the sights, sounds, smells and textures? Here are some cue questions to help people access this awareness for their life history writing.

Think about your family, about the people with whom you grew up. What was the tone of your family? Was yours a warm family? Was it loving? Peaceful? What sort of relationship did you have with your parents? What kinds of advice did your parents give you?

Did you have brothers and sisters? What was your relationship with them like? How is your relationship with them today? To whom were you closest? What are some of your favorite memories of them?

What part did religion play in your growing up? What were some of the traditions that have been handed down through your family?

Do you see any major differences between your childhood and that of your children? How did your childhood affect the way you raised your own children?

Trigger words

Following are words which can trigger long-ago memories. Ask people to choose one word and write about it as freely as possible for ten to fifteen minutes. Offer only a few words per session and have people share their writing with the group.

school	vacations	ice man
home	family	work
friend	relatives	Christmas
love	vaudeville	wash day

Negative Reminiscences And The Role Of Writing

Creative use can be made of negative reminiscences by those with deep feelings of regret and dissatisfaction about their lives. Sharing a life story with a small group of interested others is better than sitting around and brooding over past events. Writing about the past can be healing. When painful or unresolved events are staged again in our diairies or stories, a catharsis may take place which finally allows the bad experience to be put to rest.

The poems of Thomas Hardy written after the death of his wife in the course of 1912-13 are the fruit of his own remorse and regret about the unsatisfactory way their marriage had developed. They are universally recognized to be the peak of his literary achievement.

Writing The Life History In Groups

Life history writing has several positive results in group settings. Individuals who share their life stories with each other learn to appreciate the uniqueness of each life. Sharing life stories is a valuable interpersonal learning experience, as individuals receive feedback on how they are perceived by other people.

Life history groups establish a sense of fellowship. Empathy develops when painful experiences are related in a group situation and people discover that they are not alone in their feelings of disappointment, fear or joy about life events. Barriers come down and the sense of isolation gives way to a sense of shared experience.

Guidelines for Writing In Groups

- Keep work periods short and stories brief in the beginning, so that people don't tire and see writing as a task or chore. Do your best to make it into a positive, uplifting experience.

- Some people will have an abundance of themes in mind for their writing, while others will need more guidance in selecting themes.

- For those who find writing difficult, suggest the story center around events related to, for example, family life, a childhood experience, memories of schooldays or their first job.

- If writing comes hard, suggest that the person tell the experience to you first and then you may be able to help him record it as you tell it back to him.

- Build trust. People need to know that their stories will be received in a warm, supportive environment and that they will not be judged. An atmosphere of genuine trust and intimacy must be created if people are to share their lives.

"My past defines me, together with my present and the future that the past leads me to expect. What would I be without it?"

V. Neisser, 1978

Life Line

Plotting one's life line helps to chart changes and growth and to put life events into persepective. It gives people a new way of looking at the trends or directions in their lives. In much the same way as an electrocardiogram plots a heartbeat on paper, your life line plots the beat of your life on paper, in graph form.

How To Make A Life Line

You need a large sheet of white paper and a colored pen or magic marker.

- Draw a horizontal line across the center of the page. This is the time line. Divide it into five-year segments, from birth to the present.

- Go through each 5 year segment, and mark in the highs and lows for the period. A line is drawn to connect the ups and downs during each five-year period. The peaks and dips are marked with the events they signify and these ups and downs can then be explored by writing their story.

- The story may be filled in with drawings, photos, poems, and newspaper clippings.

It's possible to use different lines for different aspects of life, adding more detail and persepctive to the life line. Use one graph and one sheet of paper, but use different colored pens or pencils for the various aspects of life. For instance, maybe the famly line (blue) was moving in a very positive directions, while life's work (green) had many negative events. At the same time, health (red) was having both ups and downs.

The Future

People can continue plotting the life line into the future. While the life line to date is a solid line, a dotted line can be used to continue the life line into future years. This will be somewhat similar to an uncompleted road drawn on a map.

If you know of certain events coming up in your future, you can plot them on your graph and label them. How does your future look with these events tentatively pencilled in?

Discussing The Life Line

Spend some time discussing the life line, using these cue questions:

What was the highest point in your life?

What was the lowest?

Do you have more positive events than negative ones?

Are there any plateaus in your life line?

Any smooth periods with no highs or lows?

Are you surprised when you look at your life line?

Do you think it's a good overall picture of your life?

What is the most striking thing about it?

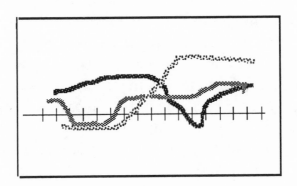

Life line

"It is extraordinary how music sends one back into memories of the past."

George Sand

Music

Music stirs memories of the past and sets the stage for a bygone era. From the first lullaby to jump rope jingles to love songs, music plays a part in everyone's life. Particular songs become associated with special times. Music communicates to us on a level more meaningful than words and draws people together in joy and community. Memories, present emotions, future hopes, and dreams can all be tied to music. As a result, it can be drawn on for rememberance of the past as well as celebrating present happenings.

The music that best evokes memories is that which people are familiar with from their childhood, dating, and young adult years. In those families where parents and grandparents sang and played music, the children often grew up being familiar with music from previous generations. Memories of this early music remain into old age. A novel approach is the use of this early music to stimulate memories and encourage older adults to tape their life histories.

Music Activities

The activities you choose depends on the individuals' taste and experiences. Knowing, for example, that an elderly person used to sing in a choir, attend ballet performances, operas, or concerts gives clues for ways to plan music entertainment for maximum therapeutic outcome.

Listening To Music

Listening to music can help an individual access old memories easily. Once you have identified preferred music tastes, you can supply appropriate background music.

Play a broad selection of music. For example, the then equivelant of pop music, music of the sentimental ballad type, and serious music (which is of a more timeless quality) should work well. Play folk songs and regional songs if relevent. Use humorous songs freely. Musical comedy numbers can be very evocative.

Love Songs

Listening to old love songs is popular. People can hear their own experiences through love songs; often they provide a validation of one's own triumphs and sadnesses in the court of love. Many people have a favorite love song which lasts throughout life. It may be reminiscent of a particular phase in a relationship; special moments associated with the song will help to recreate memories. Even if the music evokes a sad or poignant memory and brings tears, it may also bring healing.

Life-Span Songs

Select songs whch will stimulate memories of various stages of the life cycle: "Rock-a-bye Baby" "Schooldays" "Let Me Call You Sweetheart" "Home Sweet Home" "Memories." Listening to these songs can help people get in touch with parts of their past and help them come more alive in the present. This kind of music has great penetrating power and must be selected and used sensitively.

Music For Special Occasions

Play relevant music to stimulate memories of special holidays and occasions. Select short, positive musical numbers. Focus on a past or future holiday—for instance, marches for July 4; Irish melodies for March 17; carols for Christmas. Direct the discussion to childhood observances of the holiday, present feelings, and plans for future observance of the holiday.

Sing-Alongs

Many people have happy memories of occasions throughout their life-span when singing together was enjoyed. In pre-television days some families gathered around the piano on Sunday evenings and sang old favorites together.

When aired again, these songs awaken memories. Singing a college song, a hymn or camp fire song will stir memories of occasions and events permanently linked with the singing shared.

A successful old-time sing-along can be held with the older adult's family members and friends in the home, or with peers in a group environment. Use the following guidelines.

- Choose familiar songs. Vary the type of songs from peppy to slow, from fun to patriotic to serious. Use folk tunes, western hits, pop, jazz or broadway tunes. Avoid using too many sentimental numbers which may reinforce depression.

- Favorites will probably include patriotic numbers, state songs, school songs, Stephen Foster melodies, spirituals. Folk songs, drinking songs, and hymns are often popular. These songs have a greater sing-along impact because they have been part of group-singing experiences in the past.

- Choose songs based on a particular theme—songs dealing with vacations, the seasons, love, schooldays. Lyrics with repeated lines give people a better opportunity to join in. Because they are sung with gusto and enthusiasm, such songs as "The Battle Hymn of the Republic" "God Bless America" and "Johnny Comes Marching Home" stimulate spontaneous and joyful reminiscing.

- Keep all selections reasonably short and round off the session with two or three happy, snappy tunes.

Dancing To Music

Dancing is an enjoyable activity which has benefits as a physical excercise and a reminiscence vehicle. Even in simple "ballroom" dancing, old steps and movements are used, giving rise to memories and creating pleasure. Music for dancing should be chosen to suit the older person's taste and this can range from waltzes to folk dances. As well as straight forward dancing, you can use the following variations.

- People sometimes enjoy marching around the room hand in hand to old-time music. Perhaps this reactivates old memory traces of games played as children.

- Very simple folk dances are enjoyable and can also be performed quite well by many groups. These can be adapted to suit peoples' abilities.

- Clapping games from childhood can also be used, depending on the traditional activities known to members of the group. Elderly people sometimes enjoy watching children skipping while old skipping rhymes are recited. They can join in by clapping in time and by reciting the rhymes they recall.

Musical Games

Name That Tune is an enjoyable and easy-to-play game which stimulates memory. Here, play all or part of an old familiar melody and get people to guess the title. You can organize tunes around a theme—holiday songs, or songs to do with vacations, families or love.

Music Bingo uses cards with names of various songs written in the squares. It is played much like regular Bingo - a song is played, and players who have that song on their board mark it with a token. The player who gets, for example, five in a row, wins.

*"I wandered today to the hill Maggie
To watch the scene below
The creek and the old rusty mill, Maggie
As we used to long ago"*

George Washington Johnson

Outings

As well as being therapeutic, outings to familiar and favorite places prompt memory recall. Few experiences are as evocative as a visit to one's original homestead and this is a valuable, though nostalgic reminiscence activity. Seldom does the current scene match memories of how things used to be.

These "returns" engage older adults in sorting through memories, reflecting on their present meaning, and discerning the threads of continuity that join them to their past. Rummaging through remaining artifacts, souvenirs and heirlooms as well as public documents like wills, mortgages and birth certificates further activates the recall process.

When it's not possible to make such a visit personally, try to facilitate recall by photographs and by helping the individual make an approximate drawing of the ground plan of their home. By locating rooms, nooks and crannys, they may recall the activities and memories associated with same. By locating the furniture, they may remember whose favorite chair that was and experiences shared with that person.

The same flowing association of memories can result from a leisurely stroll through the neighborhood, past primary and secondary schools, the parish church, and the teenage hangouts. She can perhaps point out the street where she worked, a favorite ball park or beach. You can help by pointing out new developments enroute. Streets and buildings being remodelled or torn down provide great cues for reminiscing.

Visits to places of former employment such as industrial firms or factories can be arranged to help the person re-establish links with former colleagues and friends. Other places to visit include museums, antique shops and various exhibitions. A trip to the market will bring back familiar sights and sounds. Another outing bound to recall memories is the county fair or carnival, vintage car rallies or exhibitions of old ways of work.

Visit local historical monuments, sites of old battle-grounds or replicas of old settlements. Take time to discuss some of the historical facts which are represented there.

Plan a visit to the persons's grandchildren, pre-arranging that the theme of the visit will be to share reminiscences of growing up. Or, if you are working with a group of elderly people, arrange a convenient meeting time with a nearby school group for an oral history session.

"He is the happiest man who can see the connection between the end and the beginning of life."

Johann Wolfgang von Goethe

Photo Albums And Scrapbooks

Old photographs are to be used and treasured and are guaranteed to bring memories flooding back. The person's history or that of the family can be pieced together using photos. Put together an album of favorites, and it will make a wonderful browsing activity in quiet times. Albums with one or two pictures per page work best because they allow the older person to concentrate on one photo at a time without being distracted by the others. If the person is forgetful, label photos so that he will be able to identify relatives, friends and important events.

Then And Now Scrapbook

"Then and Now" activities are suitable for the home or day-care environment and are also ideal as part of an inter-generational project. Compile a pack of photographs of everyday items found about the home. Have two photographs of each object: the version in common use earlier this century and the modern equivalent with which we are familiar today.

The following antique objects contrasted with pictures of their more modern-day equivalents will provoke memories, laughter and plenty of discussion. The ads from *"good old days"* magazines or old catalogs are good sources for these kinds of pictures.

Old iron

Washboard

Oil lamp

Old radio

Bathtub

"The use of the human voice, fresh, personal, particular, always brings the past into the present with extraordinary immediacy"

Paul Thompson,
The Voice of the Past

Radio

The 1930's found radio in full bloom. It was the one true source of entertainment, providing a full realm of mystery, comedy, drama and news. Long before the advent of television, people sat in front of their radios to hear their favorite programs.

Reminiscing about some of those great old-time favorites can make a very nostalgic, though nonetheless enjoyable activity. The unforgettable sounds and images of radio are now readily available on cassette tape.

Radio And History

Try to find recordings of famous historical moments. Many libraries have recordings of great moments in political and sports history which are available for borrowing. Play excerpts one at a time, and let people identify what was happening.

Here are some examples of unforgettable social events which are sure to resonate strongly with many people:

- Live broadcast of King George V's Funeral
- King Edward VIII's abdication
- King George VI's coronation
- Hitler declares war on Poland
- Chamberlain announces war with Germany
- Roosevelt's "I Hate War" Speech
- Winston Churchill's "Give- Us- The- Tools" speech

Radio Comedy

Millions of radio listeners from 1931 to the very end of the radio era laughed and delighted at the antics of some of the favorite comedians of all time. These included old-timers such as Fiber McGee & Molly, Abbott and Costello, Jack Benny and, of course, Amos 'n Andy. The latter was one of American radio's smash hits and longest running programs, topping over 10,000 perform-ances. Listening to recordings of these old-time shows makes for a fun-packed activity.

Radio Drama

Old-time radio drama programs are also widely avail-able. Presented exactly as they were heard on radio many years ago, these bring back vivid memories. "War of the Worlds" for example, is the brilliantly conceived radio show produced by Orson Welles. It is presented on this tape exactly as it was heard on October 10, 1938, on the Mercury Theater of the Air. This is the production that shocked the nation into believing that the Earth was being invaded by outer space aliens, creating massive traffic jams in New York and New Jersey and flooding phone lines with calls from those who truly believed the events described were actually taking place. The show was brilliant radio—and America panicked. Marvelous nostalgia, this is a truly great way to reminisce and recall a by-gone era.

Hospital Radio

Many large hospitals now have their own radio station. A program based around the reminiscences of some of the patients and staff and integrated with record requests makes fascinating listening.

Radio Discussions

Discuss the early days of radio using prompts such as pictures of an old style radio set and pictures of radio personalities. *Great Radio Personalities in Historic Photos*, available from Dover Books is a wonderful resource for pictures. Copy the pictures. "Then and now" photos are especially interesting if you can find them. Here are some cue questions which will bring the golden age of radio to life.

When did you first start listening to the radio?

Tell us about some of the old shows you remember.

Did you have a favorite time for listening to the radio?

Do you remember hearing about any important political or world events on the radio?

Radio Quiz

Organize a quiz around old time radio, it's stars and shows. The following questions will get you started.

What drama series started off with the clock striking mid - night?

Who was the host of "the breakfast club?"

Who was radio's first child star?

Who was known for his fireside chats?

Who was the host of "the amateur hour?"

Which program played the top songs of the week?

Who read the funny papers every Sunday morning?

What was the name of the quiz show that had the "sixty-four dollar question?"

"Memory is the treasury and guardian of all things."

Cicero

Television and Slides

Old television programs can be selected to stimulate memories. Check the weekly programming schedule and make a chart showing the programs you think will be suitable. Tape this chart to the wall next to the TV set, as a reminder for the individual of suitable viewing.

Early Television

Have people share their memories of the early days of television. Find out if they recall the old television sets with the small screen and large cabinet. Show them pictures of the small pocket televisions and the giant screens of today.

Use trigger materials: pictures of old-time television personalities such as Lucille Ball, Sid Caesar and Edward Murrow. Ask people to identify the stars and tell what they remember about their shows.

Here are some cue questions about the early days of television:

Did you have a nickname for television?

Was it the Boob Tube?

When did you first see a television?

What were your favorite shows?

What was the first show you ever saw?

What historical events do you remember seeing on TV?

What programs do you like to watch these days?

Silent Movies

Talk about the silent films of old. Find pictures of the stars of the silent screen, pass them around and have people match the face with the movie. Find out who their favorites were. Charlie Chaplin, Mary Pickford, Douglas Fairbanks, Erroll Flynn and Rudloph Valentino will probably be among those chosen.

Talk about some of the great silent films of all time: "The Sheik of Araby," "The Little Tramp," "The Hunchback of Notre Dame," The Thief of Baghdad." Find out what people remember about them.

The first full-length film that had sound was "The Jazz Singer" starring Al Jolson. Find out if people remember it. Discuss how it meant the end of silent films.

Video

VCR equipment makes it possible to view films at opportune times without commercial interruptions. If you have a VCR, rent some of the old movies and arrange a special family night for viewing them every so often. Keep these points in mind:

- The shorter the movie and the simpler the story, the better.

- Silent movies are good because they tend to be short and easy to follow.

- Bright and colorful musicals, with simple story lines, also work well.

- Comedies are very popular. Try to find videotapes of old comedies by the Marx Brothers, Lucille Ball, Bob Hope, Jack Benny, Charlie Chaplin and others. Many of these can be rented at your nearby video store.

Slides

Slides have many advantages. They are effective in setting a mood, and *you* have the advantage of being able to control the pace, unlike other mediums such as TV. Slides offer a high quality image which is still and large and this is a major advantage to people who may be visually impaired.

Family slides, taken when family members were younger, provide excellent 'memory triggers' and 'then and now' comparisons. Slides of local places, churches, shopping centers, animals, pets, birds and weddings will all be of interest.

Consider having interesting family photos turned into slides. This can be done easily and means that the whole family can view them easily. People will be thrilled to see images of themselves and their families projected on the screen. There are also many interesting slide sets available commercially.

"Only when we understand where we have been, can we decide where we wish to go. And the pilgrimage continues to the moment of life's end."

E. B. Adams, 1979

Reading

Reading stirs memories. The books we read in our early days stay with us through life and returning to them in later years uncovers memories of past times. Books by Mark Twain, Robert Louis Stevenson, Dickens, the Brontes and many others are now available in large type, specially printed for older adults to read. Subjects focusing on past events such as moving house, getting married or graduating help people recall similar episodes in their own lives. Reading activities can take a variety of forms: the older adult can read by themselves or be read to by friends or family or reading can take place in a group environment.

When choosing material, for this as in other activities, keep in mind the older adults tastes and background. Look in your library for the material or contact your local bookstore for information on large type books.

Discovery Through the Humanities Series is one of the best large type selections available. These books are not only fascinating, but are also easy to read. Each title focuses on a single topic, and is made up of an introductory chapter, followed by selections from art and literature that suggest topics to think and talk about. Provocative questions accompany each inclusion.

Look in your library or bookshop for local history books documenting changes within the community—these are powerful evokers of memories. Many of these are 'then and now' books and are well illustrated with photographs which document changing traditions in the community. Such pictorial books encourage reminiscence discussion. You might ask leading questions like:

"Do you remember the skating rink?"

"Did you go there?"

Local oral history books are now available in many areas and these are ideal for reading aloud to an older adult. They can produce fascinating reminiscences which will resonate strongly with listeners, many of whom may have similar stories to tell.

Old books which were popular long ago work well for reminiscence. The *Old Farmer's Almanac* which has been published every year since 1792 is familiar to most. Each edition features astronomical information as well as games, recipes, stories, puzzles, history, astrology, contests to enter and worldly wisdom. Browse through the book with the older adult and read aloud sections which are likely to prompt memories.

Old comic strips are useful. You can find reprints of them in *Good Old Days*. Also, many libraries have books about old comics. Several of the old comic strips like "Archie", "Donald Duck", "Blondie", "Snuffy Smith", "Prince Valiant" and "Dennis the Menace" are still popular.

Copies of old newspapers are powerful reminiscence tools, especially ones with memorable headlines like "LINDBERGH LANDS IN PARIS", "THE WAR IS OVER." A reminiscence kit of famous newspaper front pages is available (see appendix 3).

Autobiographies and life stories are popular and long-forgotten memories are jogged when listening to other life tales. We often hear: *"That reminds me of when I was in school...when I was at that age....when I lived in Europe."*

Poetry also makes for pleasant reading. Since it encourages reverie and captures the emotional tone of scenes from the past, it can be used as an avenue for reminiscence. Anthologies of British and American poetry contain selections which may prompt and enrich the reminiscing process.

Also worth bearing in mind are audio books. Books and stories which are recorded on cassette tape are particularly useful for people with failing sight. Most of the classics are now available on audio tape.

Guidelines For Group Reading Sessions

Group reading sessions are often therapeutic, giving rise to distant memories and prompting people to share. The reader should be one who enjoys reading out loud, has a good strong, pleasant voice, and who uses good enunciation and diction.

Following are some guidelines to keep in mind:

- Choose reading material which is easily interpreted and plays on past experiences or events. Illustrate the selection with an object or picture and encourage people to talk about how the selection made them feel.

- Keep the selection brief to accommodate the attention span and available energy of members. Plan for one-half hour or less of reading and complete it at one session.

- Short poems and very short prose excerpts are most appropriate. One or two pages is enough; a long piece with particular appeal can be broken into sections. Each fragment can then be read and discussed separately.

- Read simple, understandable excerpts consisting of clear, everyday language and concrete images. Familiar images and events are important. Difficult passages are intimidating and distracting.

- Style and subject matter that are distasteful or offensive will destroy the possibility of discussion. Select carefully!

- Selections should have some emotional content to stir memories and generate discussion of feelings. Subjects or themes of personal relevance, such as family or friendship, are effective.

- Read the selection slowly, at your leisure. Enunciate clearly and use a good deal of expression. Dramatize with gestures, an item of costume, or a prop.

"The old are the primary link with the past—with history—for younger generations."

Page Smith, 1990

Children and Reminiscence

Reminiscence makes an ideal intergenerational activity and helps to strengthen the bond between older and younger people. It is perhaps the ultimate medium for linking generations and preserving the thread of continuity in society.

Intergenerational programs represent an extraordinary opportunity for children to share their elders' memories of childhood, family life, holidays, school days, traditions, games and other life experiences. The sharing of these treasures links today's children with yesterday's children in a common bond.

The young also gain an understanding of who they are through their connections with the past. Through reminiscing, negative stereotypes are broken down . Children come to realize that we each have a valuable history and that the history of older people is especially rich and interesting.

In turn, intergenerational reminiscing boosts the elderly person's self-esteem and makes her aware of the uniqueness and value of her individual life.

Reminiscing During Visits

Reminiscence can be used as an activity when children come to visit older adults in their own homes, day care centers or nursing home. Often the elderly person will relate more spontaneously to a young person than to an adult. The individual can be encouraged to recall experiences from the past: describe a favorite childhood room, game or set of clothing. An inexpensive tape recorder —invaluable as an aid to capturing family history— can be brought along.

Reminiscing In Schools

Many schools have begun intergenerational programs involving nursing homes and more and more teachers are building novel teaching units around reminiscence. They are capitalizing on the fact that older people are a prime source for first-hand historical knowledge about their communities.

Some schools use reminiscence activities as a focal point for *Senior Citizens Month* during which relatives or close family friends are invited to the school to spend time with children. They bring family documents, scrapbooks, passports, birth, naturalization and marriage papers, old photos and maps to show where they came from or once lived. Occasionally, they bring handcrafts from those places where they were born.

Students research in advance the visitors' countries of origin, their history and culture so that they can fully participate in the gathering. They study the period in which their elders grew up and read in advance books about the Depression and the Wars. Then they hear directly from the visitors what it was like to live though these historical periods.

Life Histories

Young people love to hear stories about life in another era, before computers, television, and men walking on the moon. Because of their natural curiosity about the past, they can create fascinating histories of the lives of their elders by tape recording the reminiscing sessions. Through the elders' eyes, they can capture a sense of times gone by—times that will never come again. For preparation, they can be encouraged to read the many pictorial historical books available as an introduction to the "old days" and discuss their reading with the older person who may be able to shed some light on certain aspects.

They can prepare questions beforehand and write them on cards. Here are some examples:

When and where were you born?

Where did you live? What games did you play?

What are some of your favorite childhood memories?

What was your greatest adventure?

Do you remember any especially funny or sad stories that happened to you in your life?

Do you recall any favorite family stories or sayings? What are they?

What were your parents like?

How much schooling did you have?

What was your favorite subject?

What did you like doing most as a child?

The best questions are those made up by the children themselves and which reflect what they want to learn from their elders. The recorded stories make fascinating listening for both young and old people. Tapes can also be transcribed and the pages may be bound in book form.

The Foxfire Projects

Many high-school students are taking reminiscence one step further by preserving disappearing knowledge and skills through *"Foxfire"* projects. *Foxfire* began at Rabun GapNacoochee High School in Georgia when a young English teacher decided his classes needed a change. He assigned his students to interview, photograph and write about the old-timers living in the Appalachian Mountains. From the material they gathered the students created a magazine.

Georgia's *Foxfire* project has now produced a series of books and inspired schools across the country to start similar programs. *Foxfire*-style projects often are part of a school's English classes, and their goal is to produce a professional-looking magazine based on student interviews with old-timers. Students in Maine, for example, publish *Salt*, a magazine crammed with interviews with fishermen, farmers and foresters.

In Alaska, high school students talked with Eskimos about arctic life 50 years ago. Navaho teenagers in New Mexico are preserving their Indian culture by producing a magazine that covers everything from moccasin-making and hair-braiding to Navaho poetry and art.

Learning Skill

Students often learn the skills they record. In a Montpelier, Vermont project, four girls began interviewing a 90-year old weaver and ended by taking weaving lessons from her. In Missouri, four girls with an interest in weaving rag rugs found experienced weavers who not only described the craft but gave them step-by-step instructions. From an old Vermont hill farmer, other students learned to "Sugar-tap" a maple tree for sap and then boil it down into maple syrup.

Sharing Sensory Experiences

When young and old work close together on sensory based activities, interactions evolve naturally. Experiences like baking or working with clay are valuable sensory tools that can tap remembrances and promote contact between the generations. Looking at old-time crafts of interest such as weaving, pottery, basket and candle-making reactivates memories. Older adults may need these kinds of hands-on activities to help remind them of their rich past.

"We reach back to the past...through reactions, impressions and moods. In so doing, we are getting a glimpse of history not made, but being made."

Imbert Orchard,
Sound Heritage

Theatre and Reminiscence

Theatrical work has been successful with elderly people and by participating in such, the individual can:

- Find satisfaction in expressing herself
- Find temporary relief from the present through playing another role
- Feel a sense of worth

In Reminiscence Theatre, the focus is on *acting out* little scenes from the past, like a visit to a Lyons tea shop, music hall scenes or riding in a Model T. This type of performance is not only rewarding to those who participate but gains the most appreciated audience response.

The active participation of the old person in the process can be a particularly powerful trigger. As well as stimulating memory, these sessions help people recover some of the social skills they have lost, particularly the ability to listen and communicate with others. Reminiscence theatre is an ideal activity for group work, either in day care or in a nursing home.

To stage your own reminiscence show:

- Encourage people to share funny, frightening or interesting anecdotes from their past. These may then be written and adapted for the theater group. Alternatively, the skits may be written from excerpts recorded during a reminiscence session.

- Create plays that are not too long and that do not require more actors than are available.

- Use relatively short scripts, skits or readings rather than complete plays. For example, you could stage a Hollywood party by having people dress as past movie stars or put on skits mimicking their favorite stars.

- If you would rather use a ready-made script, there are many skits available commercially. BiFolkal Productions' skits (see appendix 9) are written to bring back memories and encourage discussion about a time or topic in the past. The skits are in large-print and because they are short and don't require any strenuous action, they are suitable for seniors.

- "Cue cards" can be used with large-print reminders.

Local theatre groups, whether professional or amateur, can also adapt the reminiscences of seniors to the stage. In England, the *Age Exchange Theatre* Trust is a theatre company specializing in producing shows and exhibitions based on the reminiscences of older people. Based in south east London, it draws on a pool of actors, musicians, researchers, writers, designers, and reminiscence workers who have a commitment to reminiscence and community theatre.

The actors visit elderly people, and by using a range of stimuli such as photographs, music, slides and old household objects, they encourage groups of older people to reminisce. Then they record their memories.

On the basis of the collected memories, the actors devise, write and rehearse a theatrical show. (*Across the Irish Sea* is one such production which recorded the reminiscences of Irish pensioners living in London). At a later date, they return to perform it to the people whose memories have created it. This gives them the opportunity to work closely with care staff and to suggest ways in which they might continue to provide reminiscence work with their clients. A tour then follows to other local homes, day centers and sheltered housing units.

"Nothing awakens a reminiscence like an odor"
Victor Hugo

Reminisce
With Recipes

Food invokes a variety of feelings and memories and food preparation can be an extremely meaningful activity to former housewives who have spent a good part of their lives in the kitchen. The sounds, smells and tastes of the kitchen often bring back happy memories of times spent with family and friends. The distinct smells of cooking and baking can literally transport many older adults back in time to their own or neighbors' kitchens where they first sniffed these delights.

In the old days the daily diet resulted from days and months of growing, preserving, and preparing the basic foodstuffs. The woman who "set a good table" was admired in the communtiy and was a source of pride to her family and to herself. Almost all food preparation was done in the home. Bread was baked several times a week, and some cooks prepared pies every day.

A cooking session using old-fashioned recipes is sure to stimulate discussion and memories. Making ice-cream brings to mind the old days when a good helping of ice cream could be bought for five cents or memories of the winter when ice cream was often made from snow. People will recall neighborhood ice cream parlors and other associated memories like milk deliveries and licking the cream at the top of the bottle.

A bar-be-cue will bring back memories of family gatherings, camping trips and organizations such as Girl Scouts or leading a Scout trip. Making popcorn will bring back memories of munching one's way through old movies, while boiled hot dogs echo of exciting times at the ball park — with lots of mustard and relish!

Older adults might like to assist you in preparing the following recipes or might even have a few of their own from long ago. Ask if they have recipes for special dishes or baked foods that were a tradition in their family.

Rutabagas

Two generations ago, everyone raised rutabagas (sometimes called 'swedes' or 'swede turnips'). Large piles of them were stored in cool, dark basements each fall, right alongside potatoes, cabbages, squash and pumpkins. Country cooks prepared them at least once a week and never failed to include at least part of one in their vegetable soup. Here's a simple recipe using rutabagas.

Cook 4 cups of rutabagas in a small amount of boiling water until tender, 15-20 mins. Drain well

and sprinkle with a dash of salt and pepper.
Slice 1 medium onion and saute in 2 Tbs of butter
until tender. Add 1 cup sour cream to the onions
and stir well. Pour mixture over cubed rutabaga
and sprinkle with caraway or dill.

Sauerkraut

Sauerkraut was probably the first food to travel around
the world. In autumn you could count on a trip to
Grandmother's cellar to sample the kraut working mys-
teriously in the big crock. Grandmother's kraut had a
wide variety of uses from stuffing pork or poultry to
baking a cake. Here it can be used to make a simple but
nutritious salad.

Drain 2 cups finely chopped sauerkraut. Chop
half-cup each of 1 onion, celery, green pepper and
pimiento. Mix with sauerkraut. Blend in salad dress
ing of your choice. Marinate for an hour or longer.
Serve chilled.

Vanilla Ice Cream

With its invention in 1846, homemade ice cream became common in country kitchens everywhere. Hidden in the memories of long-past summer days, there is a hand-cranked ice-cream freezer on the back porch of many childhood homes. This simple recipe will bring it all back!

Combine 11/2 cups sugar, 1/4 cup flour and a dash of salt in a large saucepan. Stir in 2 cups of milk. Cook over medium heat, stirring constantly until mixture thickens and bubbles for one minute. In a large bowl beat 4 eggs. Stir half the saucepan mixture into the beaten eggs and blend well. Stir back into remaining mixture in saucepan. Cook, stirring, for one minute. Pour into a large bowl. Stir in 4 cups of heavy cream and 1tbs vanilla. Chill for at least 2 hours.

Cookies

Cookies, always popular in country kitchens can be as plain or fancy as you want to make them. The homey aroma of these fresh from the oven snacks echoes of a distant time.

Many people will recall the introduction of America's most popular cookie, the chocolate chip which swept the nation back in 1939. It was introduced to homemakers on a radio series called "Famous Foods From Famous Places." The cookie from the New England Toll House, in Whitman, Massachusetts, enjoyed immediate and continued popularity in country kitchens. Here's a simple recipe.

Heat oven to 375 degrees.
Beat 3/4 cup soft butter, 1 cup of brown sugar and 1/2 cup granulated sugar, 1 egg, 1 tsp vanilla and 2 tbs of milk together until creamy.
Sift together 1 cup flour, 1/2 tsp salt and 1/2 tsp baking soda. Add to creamed mixture, blending well. Stir in 2 cups rolled oats, 1 cup chocolate pieces and 1/2 cup of chopped nutmeats.
Drop spoonfuls of mixture onto greased cookie sheets.
Bake in pre-heated 375 degree oven 12 to 15 minutes. Makes 4 dozen.

Soda Bread

Breadbaking is as old as civilization itself and the tantalizing aroma of home-baked breads gives rise to pleasant recollections. To most people, the unmistakable smell of freshly baked bread, piping hot from the oven, brings back nostalgic memories of childhood days in country kitchens.

Homemakers of old developed their baking talents out of necessity, sometimes turning out up to five big loaves a day. Many of these were steamed in bread molds which are family heirlooms today. Later they were cooked in the huge ovens of big old-fashioned cookstoves. These rarely had thermometers, so it was a matter of 'feeling' the temperature. Bakers rarely used recipes other than pinches and handfuls. Here's a more modern but simple recipe.

Mix 2 cups whole wheat flour, 1/2 cup wheatgerm, dash salt and 3 Tbs sugar. Add 1 tsp baking powder and 3/4 tsp baking soda. Blend together.
Knead in 3 Tbs of butter.
Stir in 3/4 cup milk.
Mix well and turn into greased baking dish.
Bake in preheated oven at 350 degrees for 40 minutes.

Buttermilk Pancakes

Steaming pancakes with melted butter and maple syrup are an old-fashioned American breakfast. They are so popular that they even have a special day, Shrove Tuesday, set aside for them. On this day, before the start of Lent, people traditionally serve pancakes. It was the day to use up all the milk, eggs, and fat, which were not allowed during the strict days of Lent.

Combine 2 well-beaten eggs and 2 cups butter milk in large bowl.

Sift together 21/2 cups of white flour, 1 tsp baking soda, 2 tbs baking powder, 1 tsp salt and 2 Tbs sugar.
Stir into egg mixture.
Blend until smooth.
Add melted butter.
Drop on hot griddle.
Brown on both sides.
Serve hot with maple syrup.

Resource:

The Fannie Farmer Cookbook by Amy and Peter Pastan (Hall). This classic was first published in 1896 but its 500 recipes have been updated for this Large Type edition Older cooks will find their favorite recipes here.

"We live life forward, but understand it backward."

Kierkegaard

Reminiscence Displays

The making of a reminiscence display is a wonderful activity which gets others involved in the pasts of elderly people. The display need not be elaborate and can consist of personal belongings, objects and mementos. Local museums, antique shops or historical societies may be willing to lend items of interest. These can then be arranged as an exhibition which will help stimulate memories in the care facility.

This kind of display is also an educational experience for children and forms an interesting passive activity suitable for older people not capable of engaging in more active games. Following are ideas for simple reminiscence displays.

Photo display

Exhibitions of old photographs are always popular. This is an ideal group activity because everyone can make a contribution. You may want to choose themes under which the pictures can be arranged—eg., family, farm life, sport. Peoples' comments can be recorded and made into captions to accompany the photos. Approximately 30 photos, enlarged to standard size, is sufficient.

Our Town

Make an exhibit of changes that have occurred in the community. You could do this with old and recent photos or drawings of landmarks in the town such as old buildings, monuments, landscapes and other interesting sites. These might be obtained from the town or city hall, library or historical society. You can also make your own drawings, or 3 dimensional models with paper, papier mache or natural materials.

This is an excellent intergenerational project.

Work

Help the older person assemble objects representative of his past work life. Looking at them will help rekindle memories. They will also act as a launching point for discussion of this most important aspect of the person's past.

Through the co-operation of family members, a Lifetime Art and Craft show could display items made by various residents during their lives. This could prove to be a very interesting display for a community event such as an open house.

Other Ideas For Displays

Numerous other topics make interesting displays. Following is a partial list.

> *fashion*
> *sports*
> *the Depression*
> *carnivals*
> *big bands*
> *weddings*
> *furniture*
> *postcards*
> *farm days*
> *fairs*
> *politics*
> *war*

"By the crowd they have been broken; by the crowd shall they be healed."

L. Cody Marsh, (1935)

Reminiscing In Groups

Reminiscence can take place in any group setting where people meet for 30 to 60 minutes on a regular basis. This is an ideal activity for day care centers, senior centers and nursing homes. The activity is mainly conversational, with people recounting stories and events from the past. Reminiscing in groups provides many benefits not readily available in other contexts:

- Groups gives a sense of belonging and help to promote cohesiveness. Social bonds become strengthened when people find they have connections with others in the group, such as attending the same school or working for the same company.

- Groups also provide opportunities for memory stimulation not readily found in other settings. One person's memory can serve as a "retrieval cue" which activates latent long-term memories in others.

- One of the most satisfying aspects of reminiscing in groups is that elderly people have an opportunity to actively contribute. Through sharing experiences, they make a positive contribution towards local historical knowledge. This is in sharp contrast to much group work which places the elderly in a dependent and recipient role.

- Reminiscing together gives older people a sense of their historical influence and their legacy to society, solidifying their sense of importance and accomplishment.

- Through looking at each other, smiling, touching and holding hands, people sometimes begin to recover some of the social skills they have lost. The meetings also help rekindle a sense of belonging and connection even when speech and general coginition may have declined.

Preparing For Group Reminiscence

Familiarize yourself with each individual's life history, interests, social and cultural history and the era in which they grew up. Have some knowledge about their birthplace, where they went to school, their parents, friends, events and other early memories. Your resident files should have some of this information. If not , family and close friends will be helpful resources.

Since you may have major age differences within each group, read up about each generation separately.

Remember it is not your role to be an expert on the past. Indeed a degree of ignorance on your part is often a boost to others' confidence and also draws out more reminiscence.

Gather items that relate to birthplaces: pictures, things made there, information about what the place is famous for. Books dealing with the growing up years stimulate memories.

The Reminiscence Room
Find a quiet room. People need to feel relaxed and un-pressured if they are to reminisce comfortably, and a colorful, warm, and relaxed atmosphere can help.

It is helpful to create as much of the home atmosphere as possible. Small considerations in room layout and design can spell the difference between success and failure within a group. Wall space for displaying posters provides a visual means of recollecting previous sessions, and so builds continuity. Chairs should be arranged in a semi-circle around the table on which materials for the session are displayed. One or two chairs with arms are useful to support any elderly patients who may tend to tilt to the side or fall asleep.

Group Members
Mixed Groups.

Try grouping together people who are at a similar level of functioning. A mixed group may not be able to meet the needs of all its members; some may become bored while others feel left behind. Also, it is upsetting for the less confused to be classified with those whom they consider worse than themsleves.

Mixing men and women.
It's not necessary to separate men from women. In fact it is much better to combine the two. After all, their past has included both males and females and there is a better social exchange when both sexes are present. Being part of a mixed group may be an added incentive to take an interest in clothes and appearance.

Some people, however, feel more comfortable in same-sex groups. This is particularly the case with those who grew up with taboos forbidding them from sharing intimacies with the opposite sex. Only after meeting with potential members will you be able to assess preferences here.

If the group *is* mixed, be alert to the numbers of men and women, so that either a man or woman on his or her own does not feel overwhelmed or left out.

Consistency
Consistency and continuity with respect to time, place and member participation are essential features of a successful group. Plan to meet at the same time each week for a specified length of time — the optimum duration of meetings is from thirty to forty-five minutes, but this will vary depending on who is involved and the nature of the discussion.

Group Size

The optimum group size depends on peoples' abilities and the amount of support they require. If members are confused, the group can be limited to two or three people, although two leaders may be able to cope with four or five people. If people are very confused, consider working on a one-to-one or one-to-two basis.

Where group members are alert, you can work comfortably with up to eight people. Feel free to experiment and find the size you can cope with. Consider taking 2 to 4 people initially and getting to know them before you gradually add more — thus building up to the desired class size.

Try to limit the group size to ten people. Large groups easily lose the personal element of sharing experiences as reticent members may be hesitant to contribute. Also, some individuals may have difficulty hearing or taking an active part in large groups.

The Group Leader

A good group leader is, in essence, a facilitator. Historical knowledge is not essential — more important qualities are enthusiasm, imagination and sensitivity to how groups operate

- A group leader must be able to develop a trusting relationship with each participant so that she will feel trusting enough to invest something of herself, become involved and feel good about herself.

133

- Good leadership involves controlling discussion and encouraging everyone to participate. This means being firm with people who talk too much, who go off the subject, or who try to engage the person sitting next in a separate conversation. It's equally important to be aware of withdrawn people and seek sensitive ways of involving them.

- The group leader takes on the job of trying to find topics or memory makers that will be meaningful to members and prompt some form of participation. After that, the group can often find a life of its own.

The sessions are often highly enjoyable and informative as people recount a wealth of informative stories and memories of happy days. You may be surprised by what these people can teach you about their own times and their way of life.

Co-leadership

Consider running the group with a co-worker. You can then support each other and generate ideas together. One person can sometimes take an observational role, monitoring progress. Or the co-leader can take notes and this information can be filed and used for future sessions.

Life-Span of Group

Decide how long the group will continue to meet. Some groups meet together for five years or more without running out of new ideas to explore, but reminiscence can also be organised on a much shorter term basis, even for 6 sessions.

Running The Group

The session begins with a small circle of people. The circle helps people feel closer to each other, and it also offers good visibility and reduces anxiety. Socialization with other group members is encouraged so there is an opportunity to touch and make eye contact.

Put together those people from the same area or part of town or those with similar past hobbies or occupations. Take into consideration hearing or speech problems, mannerisms or habits. A reasonably chatty person needs a neighbor to hear and respond to her conversation. Alternatively she could be placed to stimulate a more withdrawn person to interact.

Seat yourself in the middle around the table so that everyone can see and hear you. Don't use a microphone unless necessary as it may take away some of the group's spontaneity. If group members are hard-of-hearing, you may have to use a mike.

Invite everyone to introduce themselves, giving help where necessary. Even if people live together, the chances are great that they do not know one another's names or that they may have forgotten them. A good exercise is to have each resident say his name and shake hands with the person on both sides. Hearing the name reinforces it in the mind of the neighbor, and shaking hands is an opportunity for social contact.

Introduce the topic for discussion. Say: *"I'm interested in how you feel about this,"* or *"Does this bring any memories to you?"* If people are from various parts of the country, ask each individual to tell a little about the place where she grew up. As a cue, you could get a map of the United States and put labels where each resident was born.

Encourage group members to contribute their stories. In doing so, remember that people are sharing a part of themselves and they may feel somewhat vulnerable after this. Different groups will set their own pace — some may like a leisurely unfolding of memories — so there is no need to be embarassed by a silence or pause while people reflect on what they have seen or heard. A light remark can help the silence from becoming oppressive.

Some people will be content to just sit in the group without actively participating. You can try coaxing them into the discussion with questions. For example, " John, did you hear what Mary just said?"
The best endings usually include some humor: sharing a joke, a cartoon or comic strip. Serving light refreshments is also a great way to end. Warmly thank each person for coming and for helping you get to know a bygone era. Let them know that you have found them interesting and informative and that you are looking forward to meeting them again.

Tell them what the next discussion topic will be, for example, *"We will talk about your first dance the next day."*

In the interim, everyone will have a chance to think about the topic and memories will be stirred of things long forgotten. By the time the meeting comes around, people may recall past experiences in considerable detail.

Special Issues

Honoring Privacy

Each person has the right to privacy, to not share a particular theme with the group if the topic is too sensitive or painful. This may only happen occasionally, but when people do express a desire to pass on a given subject, their wishes should be respected. No one should feel forced to share everything.

The Need for Flexibility

Be prepared to change plans. Some days are conductive to singing or active games. You will learn to recognize these days and change your plans accordingly. What takes place depends on the atmosphere created by the whole group and the flexibility of individuals present.

Guidelines

- Go slowly—both in speech and movement.
- Allow silent ones to participate at their own pace.

- Keep your questions short and open-ended–for example, *"I can't imagine living without electricity; how did you read at night?"*
- Sit beside nervous or agitated members or the most confused.
- Let people teach you. They have a need to be needed.
- Use physical contact—for example, hand touch, leg tap, hug.
- Expect some sad topics. Do not discourage them.
- Draw out quiet ones in a gentle way.
- Help keep facts accurate by relating them to the past as opposed to the present.

Problems

Clashing Personalities

There will always be clashing personalities within the group and you will have to manage these people as the situation arises. Later when you know a person's idiosyncrasies or dislikes you can forestall irritating situations by placing them strategically as they arrive for class.

Domination

It's okay to let a person dominate a group as long as it's not the same person every week. Where one or two people tend to dominate the group *consistently*, you will need to find ways to let each individual contribute. Make it clear that people should take turns and listen to each other. Allow only one person to talk at a time and gently discourage others from carrying on conversations while another is talking. Don't let this come across as a rebuke but rather as an interest in what each individual has to share.

Repetition

If someone comes up with the same story repeatedly, think hard about how you can get them to develop the story further. It may be possible to ask some detailed questions or ask them to explain an aspect of the story.

Instead of cutting the person off abruptly, gently say something like:

"I remember when you told us that. It must have been a very special moment for you." Then add, *"I'd like to hear you talk about..."* and choose some part of the person's life with which you are not familiar.

Pay close attention to those stories the person repeats again and again. They may be special and may give a clue to some agitiation or special joy the person is feeling.

Listlesness

If someone is inclined to fall asleep or wander away, look into the possible reasons. It may be an indication that the group is going on for too long, the topic may not relate to their experience or they may not be suitable for the group. Alternatively you may not have made an effort to include them in the group.

Interrruptions

Take time to listen to those who speak slowly. Don't let another more impulsive or less patient person interrupt. For example, say: *"Wait Gabriel, let John finish his story first, then you can share yours."*

Time

Time is usually the most common problem for small groups. One person may want to talk endlessly, leaving no time for everyone else. This can be avoided if there is a timekeeper for the group and if everyone knows at the outset that they have X amount of time. Fairness should be stressed, so that everyone has roughly equal time.

Judgementalism

Nothing can make the group fail faster than someone criticizing another person's life. A critical attitude on anyone's part will hurt people's feelings, destroy trust, and inhibit the group process.

The ending

Plan in advance how the final sessions will end for groups which have been set up to run for a limited period. Try to ensure that people are not being left unduly with uncomfortable feelings about the past. Also be aware that people have come to know each other intimately and because of the bonding process, they may not want to let go of each other.

One good way to ease the sadness of ending is to have a celebration at the last group meeting. A pot-luck with some old-time favorites is a fitting way to draw the sharing process to an end and makes closure easier. It sets a tone of celebration for the sharing that has taken place, enabling everyone to leave with a positive, uplifted feeling.

Another parting exercise is to have each person write out a wish for each group member and bring these wishes on the last day. By the time a reminiscence group ends, people are familiar enough with each other to make a good wish for each. The ending, however it takes place, should reaffirm each individual's life, sending people off into the future with renewed energy and enthusiasm.

Appendix 1

PERSONAL PROFILE

This profile identifies some of the key areas relating to the individual's past. It can be useful in generating ideas for reminiscence. Photocopy these pages and use copies for your work.

Name
Birthplace   **Birthdate**
Childhood History: Friends, relationships, experiences, pastimes.
Family History Number of siblings, parents'occupations, martial history, number of children, names

Nationality of Ancestors
Health History
Previous Interests & Abilities
Former Occupations
Hobbies
Musical Tastes
Clubs and Organizations
Church Preferences
Current Interests

Appendix 2

AGE CHART

This chart is a useful, quick reference for establishing the age of older people at various points in this century.

Year Born	1900	1920	1930	1939	1950	1960	1970	1980	1990
1880	20	40	50	59	70	80	90	100	110
1885	15	35	45	54	65	75	85	95	105
1890	10	30	40	49	60	70	80	90	100
1895	5	25	35	44	55	65	75	85	95
1900		**20**	**30**	**39**	**50**	**60**	**70**	**80**	**90**
1905		15	25	34	45	55	65	75	85
1910		10	20	29	40	50	60	70	80
1915			15	24	35	45	55	65	75
1920			10	19	30	40	50	60	70
1925			**5**	**14**	**25**	**35**	**45**	**55**	**65**
1930				9	20	30	40	50	60
1935				4	15	25	35	45	55

Source: Recall Review, Age Concern, England

Appendix 3

RESOURCES FOR REMINISCENCE

The following resources are designed to stimulate reminiscence and are available from Elder Press, 731 Treat Ave, San Francisco, CA. 94110.

American Lifestyles: The March of Time Videos
A boxed collection of six videos showing how Americans lived, loved, played, shopped, dressed and more, against the turbulent backdrop of the war and post-war years. Winner of over 40 awards. $160.00.

Famous Front Pages traces the major social and political landmarks of bygone years through a series of original newspaper headlines spanning the 1900's. This evocative collection comes with a 60 minute cassette tape with selected readings. $32.00.

Famous Faces include four sets of portraits of the presidents, black Americans, famous woman and movie stars. These faces from the past come with information cards, suggested activities, quizzes and trivia. $15.95 each.

Radio's Greatest Comedies contain four hour-long cassettes of the funniest comic talent ever to grace the airwaves. A treasure house of enjoyable memories. $21.95.

Big Band Gold Thirty-seven superstars of the big band era bring it all back home in four one-hour tapes. Ideal music for reminiscence. $21.95.

Appendix 4

SOURCES FOR GAMES

The games described in Section 11 are obtainable from the sources listed here.

Three Score and Ten is available from Senex Enterprises, 1506 Holly Bank Circle, Dunwoody, GA. 30338 Price: $20.00 postpaid.

Generations is available from Generations Inc., PO Box 41069, St. Louis, MO. 63141 Price: $42 postpaid.

Cross Country is available from Eldergames 11710 Hunters Lane, Rockville, MD. 20852 Price: $37.50 postpaid.

Penne Ante is available from Geriatric Resources, 5450 Barton Drive, Orlando, FL. 32807 Price: $16 postpaid.

Appendix 5

BOOKS ABOUT REMINISCENCE

These are some of the most useful books, articles and periodicals for people interested in using reminiscence and oral history.

Memories Are Made Of This, Elder Press, 731 Treat Ave, San Francisco, CA. 94110. $15 for annual subscription. A first-of-its-kind quarterly journal which focuses on reminiscence. Full of interesting activities capitalizing on the past as well as resources and personal accounts from people who use reminiscence in their work.

Reminiscence And Life Review In The Aged: *A guide for the elderly, their families, friends and service providers,* Adams, E.B. 1979. North Texas State University, Center for Studies in Aging.

Ageing and Reminiscence Processes, Coleman, P.G. 1986 New York: John Wiley and Sons.

Uses of Reminiscence: *The New Ways of Working with Older Adults,* Kaminsky, M. 1984 New York: Haworth Press.

Reminiscence, Norris, A. 1988 London: Winslow Press.

A Professional's Guide to Older Adults' Life Review: *Releasing the Peace Within,* Magee, J. 1988 Lexington: Lexington Books.

Reminiscence: *Finding Meaning in Memories*, AARP 1990, PO Box 19269, Station R, Washington, DC 20036.
Trainers' guide and resource material. Eighty slides and a 13-minute tape show the importance of memories at every age in a program called Memories: Keys to the Present.

The Voice of the Past: *Oral history*, Thompson, P. 1978 Oxford: Oxford University Press.
Probably the most widely recommended publication in the history and methods of oral history. Includes useful model question sets.

How To Tape Instant Oral Biographies, Zimmerman, W. 1988 New York: Guarionex Press.

Appendix 6

ACTIVITY BOOKS

Remembering the Good Old Days, Knoth, M 1989 IN: Valley Press.
This well researched book offers 100 topics for lively reminiscing.

Down Memory Lane, Beckie Karras, Maryland: Circle Press 1988.
This book contains ideas for small group reminiscing sessions in nursing homes.

Come and Sit by Me: *Discussion Programs for Activity Specialists,* Lausch S. G .1988 Maryland: National Health Publishing.
Organized by season, the guidelines here provide topics for reminiscence.

Let's Talk Again, Ashworth, 1987 E. CA: L'Anciana Press.
This book of remotivation programs for use in nursing homes contains many themes for reminiscence groups.

Memories, Dreams and Thoughts: *A Guide to Mental Stimulation,* Brennan, J. DC: American Health Care Ass.
This resource is full of mental stimulation games and questions for discussions.

Music and Memories, Karen Bauman NY: Potentials
Development.
This booklet has 38 topics and topic-related songs written
with words and music and is written with the music/
discussion group leader in mind.

Parkers Gazette Larry Goudge, PO Box 28444, Santa Ana
CA. 92799.
This bi-monthly magazine is suitable for activity directors
and other caregivers. A great discussion-starter. Full of
creative and informative "old news" sources.

Appendix 7

HISTORY BOOKS

The following history books help stimulate reminiscence. Many are illustrated with vivid pictures—leafing through them makes an ideal browsing activity.

A Family Album: *The American Family in Literature and History*, Alvarez, R & Kline, S. 1988 NY: Walker
Here are snapshots of the American family that make families stand still for a brief look and see what has happened to American families over the years and how they have been affected by events.

The Remembered Past: *1914-1945*, Alvarez, R & Kline, S. 1988 NY: Walker.
Photos and excerpts focus on the War to end all Wars, the Roaring Twenties, the Depression and the World at War again.

Hard Times: *An Oral History of the Great Depression*, Terkel, Studs, 1970 NY: Pantheon Books.
Perhaps noone has captured the spirit of the Thirties with such immediacy and poignancy as author and radio commentator Studs Terkel. He has interviewed people from all walks of life and recorded their memories and impressions of the chaotic and painful years of the Depression in *Hard Times*.

This Fabulous Century *1900-1970*, N Y: Time Life Books.
A compelling series of books on each one of the first six decades of the 20th century.

Only Yesterday, Allen, F. L. NY: Bantam Books, 1931.
A personal and popularized survey of the 1920's, written at the decade's close. Allen makes the period come alive.

Since Yesterday, Allen, F.L. 1940 NY: Bantam Books.
Allen treats the Thirties in similar fashion to the Twenties, covering the decade with humor and a keenly observant eye.

The Twenties: *Fords, Flappers and Fanatics,* ed. Mowry, George E., 1963.
Documentary collection dealing with the rise of mass culture in the 1920's, including articles on the rage for mah jongg, the movies, sports, Charles Lindbergh and the Ku Klux Klan. Selections originally appeared in magazines during the 1920's.

Living History, 1925-1950, by Dylong, John, 1979 Chicago: Loyola University Press.

Step It Down, by Jones, Bessie & Hawes, Bess Lomax 1972 NY: Harper & Row Publishers.

Life Goes To War: *A Picture History of World War II*, Scherman, D. 1977 NY: Time/Life Books.

Normal Rockwell books, Norman Rockwell painted hundreds of pictures that captured the spirit and culture of America. There are also many collections of his paintings available.

We The People , the National Geographic Society, Washington, D.C., 1975
This is a very good summary of American history, with many pictures and quotations.

Let Us Now Praise Famous Men, Agee, James and Walker Evans, 1939. A classic, breathtaking examination of the lives of typical sharecropper families in the South in the late 1930's. Includes Evans' unforgettable photographs.

The 1940's: *Profile of a Nation in Crisis.* ed. Eusinger, Chester, 1969. An excellent documentary anthology of the 1940's, including photos, literature, cartoons and reproductions of fine art.

An American Exodus: *A Record of Human Erosion in the Thirties,* Lange, Dorothea and P.S. Taylor 1969 Haunting visual record of the flight of farmers in the 1930's with commentary.

Life's Picture History of World War 11, Time/Life Books 1950. A good visual record of the Second World War.

Appendix 8

MAGAZINES TO AID REMINISCENCE
The following magazines focus on the old days and make nostalgic and evocative reading for seniors.

Good-Old Days
This monthly contains quaint stories, old-fashioned stunts, pictures and old ads. Presented on newsprint, it also has short, memory-sharing articles that are good for reading groups. Good Old Days P.O. Box 11302, Des Moines, IA. 50340-1302.

Scrapbook Pages
This bi-monthly publication includes pictures and stories about the past, mixed with craft projects, puzzles, poems, and items of current interest. It's printed in large-type for older readers or others who may be partially sighted. PO Box 5583, Arlington, VA. 22205.

Old Stuff
This bi-monthly, old-fashioned, historical magazine is easy to hold but has small print.
1233 Janesville Ave Fort Atkinson WI 53538.

Ideals
This magazine is full of beautiful pictures and poetry which can stimulate private reminiscence. It's also very useful in getting a discussion started.
Ideals Publishing Corporation, 11315 Watertown Plank Rd, Milwaukee, WI. 53226.

Sunshine Magazine
This monthly magazine can be obtained in large-print. It's largely human interest and inspirational in its appeal. Sunshine, Litchfield, Illinois 62056.

Memories- The Magazine of Then and Now-
This slick magazine is full of stories about events of the past, often written by eyewitnesses. Each issue features events from 20, 25, 30, 40, and 50 years ago.
PO Box 50071, Boulder, CO. 80321-0071.

Appendix 9

Oral History Association
PO Box 926,
University Station,Lexington
KY 40506-0025. Membership $20 per year.
The oldest and only national association for oral history.
Great annual journal explores developments in oral history, reviews books, etc and quarterly newsletter contains news, bibliography, events, etc.

Canadian Oral History Association
Box 301, Station A,
Ottawa, Ontario
KIN 8V3

National Archives,
Room 1111, 711 14th St NW,
Washington,
DC 20408
For assistance in getting started on genealogical research.

Bi-Folkal Productions
809 Williamson St
Madison
WI. 53703

Publishers of reminiscence resources, many of which are available through libraries.

ORAL HISTORY PROJECTS:

Indiana Homemaker Association
C/O Eleanor Arnold,
RR2, Box 48, Rushville,
IN. 46173
This oral history project has produced a six-book series of oral history books, called *Hoosier Homemaker Through the Years*. They cover the period of life from the early 1900's through WW11.

Chippewa Valley Museum Oral History Project
The contents of this oral history collection cover a period of more than 100 years, starting with stories of how inter-viewees' grandparents and parents settled the Chippewa Valley. They describe the coming of such technological wonders as bicycles, automobiles, movies, radio, farm machinery and indoor plumbing.
Contact: Project Director, Chippewa Valley Museum, PO Box 1204, Eau Claire, WI. 54702.

Elders as Consultants: The "Lifestories" Program
This is a rural, community based program by and for older persons to develop story-sharing skills and other activities. In their extensive research with church congregations, the co-directors have learned that the process of sharing life stories helps lessen loneliness and isolation.
Contact: H. Thorsheim & B. Roberts, Dept of Psychology, St. Olaf College, Northfield, MN. 55057.

Appendix 10

FILM AND VIDEO RESOURCES

Passing Quietly Through   26 minutes
A welfare nurse's visits to a dying old man in a seedy New York hotel room produce a tenuous bond between the two as they finally begin to communicate by sharing memories they previously have not shared with others. The realism and force of the "life review" process has made this an award-winning film.

Minnie Remembers   5 minutes
Minnie has only the memories of the warmth and pleasure of loving touches, kisses, and embraces from the days of her childhood, marriage, and motherhood. The film's sensitive point is beautifully made.

I'm the Prettiest Piece in Greece   30 minutes
Documentary about Billie Haywood, a black singer of cafe society in the '30's and '40's. Now living alone, Miss Haywood reminisces, sings, and shows clips from some of the films she appeared in. Film could be used for training in reminiscence therapy, although the dialogue is sometimes hard to hear.

The above films are available from:
Gerontological Film Collection Media Library, PO Box 12898, North Texas State University, Denton, TX. 76203.

Steps Back in Time   10 mins
In this film by Andrew Ruhl, an old woman reminisces about her youth. The scene is an old rehearsal hall, and the woman again becomes the young ballet dancer she once was. Hundreds of still photographs are arranged to create an effect of continuous movement. A study guide is included.
AIMS Media Inc, 626 Justin Ave, Glendale, CA. 91201.

Peege   28 minutes
This film by Peege's grandson shows the dynamics of family relationships and is an excellent example of reminiscing. Instructional Media Services 205 Milton Bennion Hall, University of Utah, Salt Lake City, UT 84112.

A Private Life
This film is about a lively, beautiful 70-year old who refuses to lose her grip on life. Her friend, Karl, a retired engineer, is writing his memoirs. As he reads his memoirs to her, he slips into reminiscence. Both are Jews who fled Nazi Germany and have painful memories. Their handling of the memories is of interest. Contact: Museum of Modern Art, Dept of Film (Attn: William Sloan), 11 West 53rd St, NY, NY. 10020.

Old Friends with Pat Keliher
This television show which emphasizes reminiscence, airs weekly over Public Access Community Television, (Cable Channel 8, Eau Claire). Its host, Martin Pat Keliher, himself a senior, reminisces with guests about by-gone

days in western Wisconsin and talks to them about their hobbies and recreational activities. Topics to date have included country schools, farm and kitchen antiques, Scandinavian culture, threshing, quilting, old-fashioned Christmases, ghost towns, and storytelling. Fascinating listening and reminiscing for older adults.

Contact Joanne Flemming, Producer, PACT, Cable Channel 8, 400 Eau Claire St, Eau Claire, WI. 54701.

Wild Strawberries
This is the story of an egocentric professor who becomes aware of his failings by a process of dreams and conscious recollection of family relationships and his place within them. As a result he is led to seek reconciliation with his estranged son and daughter-in-law.

Ingmar Bergman's film is cited both by Butler (1963) and Erickson (1978) as an example of the process of life reviewing.

Water From Another Time   29 mins.
Three older people share their memories through music, art and diaries. Reminiscence is portrayed as life enriching and the film emphasizes the value of preserving expressions of the past.

Kane-Lewis Productions, 1813 Cranberry Lane, Reston, VA. 22091.

Index

MEMORIES ARE MADE OF THIS
A Journal of Reminiscence Activities for Caregivers

This is a quarterly journal full of activities capitalizing on the past, as well as personal accounts from people who use reminiscence in their work. Both the family caregiver and the professional working in day care or long term care will find it an invaluable resource.

- An activity section in each issue presents a wide variety of illustrated activities which capitalize on the past.

- A Q & A column answers questions most often asked about running reminiscence sessions.

- A resource section advises on where to obtain useful trigger materials such as books, music and old radio shows.

> *"an excellent resource for all those involved in reminiscence work."* Resources in Aging

Published quarterly, one year's subscription to **Memories** costs $15 (see Order Form).